The Uncensored Story of a Minister's Life

*Blessings and Bruises,
Successes and Shipwrecks
Guidance and Groping,
Rewards and Regrets*

Ronald Higdon

Energion Publications
Gonzalez, FL
2024

Copyright © 2024, Ronald W. Higdon

Scripture Quotations:
Scripture quotations marked HART are taken from The New Testament by David Bentley Hart, copyright 2017 by Yale University Press, New Haven.
Scripture quotations marked MESSAGE are taken from The Message. Copyright 1993, 1994, 1995, 2000, 2001. Used by permission of NavPress Publishing Group.
Scripture quotations marked NJB are taken from The New Jerusalem Bible, copyright 1985 by Darton, Longman & Todd, Ltd. and Doubleday Dell Publishing Group Inc. All rights reserved.
Scripture quotations marked NLT are taken from the Holy Bible, New Living Translation, copyright 1996, 2004, 2007, 2013 by Tyndale House Foundation. Used by permission of Tyndale House Publishers, Inc., Carol Stream, Illinois 60188. All rights reserved.
Scripture quotations marked NRSV are taken from the New Revised Standard Version, copyright 1989 by the Division of Christian Education & the National Council of the Churches of Christ.

Cover Design: Henry E. Neufeld

ISBN: 978-1-63199-925-3
eISBN: 978-1-63199-926-0

Energion Publications
1241 Conference Rd
Cantonment, FL 32533

850-525-3916

pub@energion.com

ACKNOWLEDGMENT

My deep appreciation to Dr. John Lloyd for reading this manuscript, correcting typos, and making helpful observations. He told me that as he read, he was reminded of a poem he wrote in 2017. With his permission, here is that poem:

Roads Contemplated

If you don't know where you are going,
Any road will get you there,
But, to be where you don't belong
Will too soon lead to despair.

Some choose the road of least resistance,
But, it often leads to nowhere
Which is the same as not anywhere.
Most, surely desire to be somewhere.

Some choose the road most traveled
And join the chanting crowd.
But, success rarely comes
By only being loud.

Some choose a road of service
To the benefit of all who travel.
The course is always forward plotted.
But, that road is seldom level.

Some choose a road by careful measure
And arrive where they belong.
Is it better to choose thus wisely
Even though you may travel alone?

Table of Contents

Acknowledgment iii
Preface: The Story – True as I Remember It vii

1	Unavoidable or Uncovered 1
2	Rough Beginnings 7
3	Rural Enlightenments 11
4	You Never Know What Might Be Next 17
5	A Little Rocky in Rocky Mount 25
6	Blue Ridge Oasis 37
7	A Wider World of Opportunity and Crisis 47
8	Seven Interim Ministry Journeys 59
9	Books and Discoveries 73
10	Writing and Workshops 93

Reflections and Personal Observations 99

Bibliography of Quoted Sources 113

PREFACE

THE STORY – TRUE AS I REMEMBER IT

"One gets over everything," repeated Wimsey firmly.
"Particularly if one tells somebody about it."
"One can't always tell things."
"I can't imagine anything really untellable."[1]

NOT A DETAILED AUTOBIOGRAPHY

This book is more like snapshots of persons and events that carved themselves into my emotions and memory than a book about all that happened. In my years of visiting nursing homes, I soon learned that my most important role was not that of giving good pastoral advice for the challenge of aging, but of being a good listener who provided a safe place where nothing was really untellable.

In my early months at Broadway, I made a hospital visit with my usual opening gambit, "How is everything going?" Without hesitation, I got my answer from a woman in her late eighties: "Don't let anybody fool you. Old age is hell!" While contemplating an appropriate pastoral response, she quickly added: "Okay. Now that we have that out of the way we can have a good visit." And we did, because it was not based on anything I said but on my being a good listener. That does not come easily for me and I have to keep working on it. In all my years of college, seminary,

---

1 Dorothy Sayers, *The Unpleasantness at the Bellona Club*. (London: Hodder and Stoughton, 2003), 238.

and graduate study I had many courses on how to talk; I never had a single course on the value of being "on the listen."

Non-judgmental listening comes with no evaluations or advice, no commentary of any kind. If the elderly keep repeating their stories, it is only because they need to tell them again to someone who will listen. It seems so important that I do not understand why there has not developed somewhere along the way a "Ministry of Listening." This listening provides the unspoken blessing of affirming a life lived, its value, and its meaning. Especially as we age and those who are familiar with our stories become fewer and fewer, this would fill an ever-enlarging void. I have always believed that the church should be a safe place where every story matters and no story is untellable.

JUST THE FACTS?

In the "radio days" of my youth (many cannot imagine life without televisions and smartphones), one of my favorite shows was *Dragnet*. A memorable line came in almost every episode when the interviewing officer would caution an interrogated witness who wandered into commentary: "Just the facts, ma'am. Just the facts." I later came to realize he was asking for the impossible.

When eye-witness accounts of almost any accident are assembled, the inevitable question arises: "Are they talking about the same event?" A current read, with the arresting title *Eyes Wide Open,* gives this insight: "You do not see with your eyes, you see with your brain. The experience of sight is far more complex than perceiving what is around you."[2] When sharing "what they saw," people do not share mechanical fixed snap-shots. Perceptions and assumptions (frequently unrecognized) distort the picture that prevents it from being an image of exact reality.

My goal at the start was to read *The Papers of George Washington* in their entirety with my own eyes. Though I

2   Isaac Lidsky, *Eyes Wide Open* (New York: A TarcherPerigeeBook, 2017), 9.

achieved my goal, it quickly became apparent that other eyes would be necessary to challenge my interpretative instincts and correct my inevitable gaffes.[3]

We face the same kind of dilemma when we open our memory files to recall the events and experiences that are "stored" there. As I tell my story in this book, it is as I remember it. I must continually ask myself such questions as: Am I reading something into this that was not there? Am I substituting what I wish I had said or done for what occurred? Am I softening the sharp edges and curbing the emotions because the passage of time has done that for much in my memory bank? Time does not necessarily heal all wounds but it often has a way of lessening their impact. I usually have different perspectives and different evaluations from those of earlier and less mature times (hopefully!).

I include the word "uncensored" in the title of this book because I have made every effort to include the bitter with the sweet, the wisdom with the folly, the acceptance with the judgmental, the dedication and commitment with the self-centeredness, and the days of faith and courage with the days of fear and the desire to quit the impossible demands of being a pastor. But do not despair! As I look back on over sixty years of ministry, I do so with gratitude and thanksgiving for the opportunities that have been mine and for the countless number of truly wonderful people I have known. Even if I had been able to do so, I would not have done anything else in the world. I have had a truly blessed life – blessed not only by God but especially by those whom I was permitted to serve. In Romans 1:12, Paul wants to visit with the Christians in Rome so that *"we may be mutually encouraged by each other's faith"* (NRSV). I know what he meant; this has been my experience over those sixty years. I knew it then and the years have only strengthened and deepened that memory and conviction which I have come to believe is a large part of God's sustaining grace.

3   Joseph J. Ellis, *His Excellency: George Washington* (New York: Vintage Books, 2004), 277.

NAMES AND PLACES

All church names and places are authentic; references to specific individuals usually bear fictitious names. All the incidents given represent some of things that keep forcing their way into my consciousness as I go about minding my own business. The dates for each chapter are approximate and there is some overlapping. Psychologically, some would say they are issues that have not yet been resolved. I would contend that many of them are beyond resolution: they simply are what they are. Lessons have been learned, repairing bridges has been ongoing, and reconciliation and forgiveness have come into play when appropriate and possible.

The past is never really the past. With the least provocation, it has the habit of poking its way into present moments. Perhaps one of the major projects of old age is the reworking, rethinking, and making peace with what has been written on scrolls of our past journeys and previous experiences. This is more than simply looking back; it involves as honest an appraisal as possible and a healing and reshaping to permit a present journey without too many lingering roadblocks and potholes. Perhaps that is one of the major reasons the conclusion of this book indicates a work that continues to be in progress.

I hope this book will be one of continuing discoveries and revelations. My prayer is that this will be a mutual experience in our journey together through these pages.

The following paragraph is Dr. John Lloyd's impression as he read the manuscript. It certainly is one of my unstated intentions. To conclude this Preface, I use his words and make them mine:

> It was not (and is not) my intent in this book to write only a biographical sketch of my somewhat long, mostly successful, sometimes precarious, career in the Baptist ministry; but perhaps primarily to cite a long, reasonably successful journey that may be instructive for those considering a career in ministry.

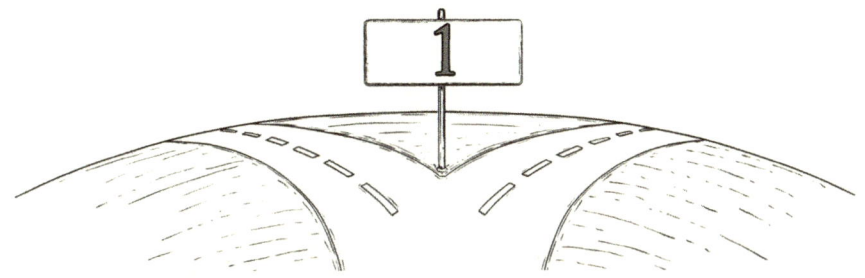

Unavoidable or Uncovered

Then Eli perceived that the Lord was calling the boy. Therefore Eli said to Samuel, "Go lie down; and if he calls you, you shall say, 'Speak, Lord, for your servant is listening.'" 1 Samuel 3:9-10, NRSV.

A TWENTY-FIVE -YEAR-OLD SECRET

I never heard a voice calling my name. I never had a burning bush experience like Moses. I never had a "knock your socks off" calling like Paul. It was only after I was married (at 25) that my wife (Pat) told me something my mother had shared with her. It was something she had never told me. In the family collection of photos, there was a picture of my parents standing beside a gravesite. They had just buried their firstborn son who died shortly after birth. My mother told Pat that on that day she had made a vow; she promised the Lord that if he gave her another son, she would dedicate him to His service. About a year and a half later, I came into the world.

As a young girl, my mother's dream was to become a missionary. That was not to be. The depression, which hit rural America with a vengeance, forced my mother to quit school after the elementary grades and go to work to help the family survive. I do not believe she intended for me to live out her dream. She never hinted that she wanted me to become a minister.

In any interview process for a prospective pastor, the inevitable question is: "Tell us about your call to ministry." My answer was always the same: I never knew a time when I did not want to be a minister. When still in early grade school, my mother related how I would arrange a couple of chairs for my two sisters (later to number three), stand before them with a Bible (mostly unreadable to me) and preach a sermon to them. I have no idea what subjects I covered or what I believed to be the purpose of my discourses, but, according to all reports, I did it with gusto.

Question: was this God's predestination working its way out in response to my mother's prayer at the grave of her first son? Was there no possible way I could not have become a minister? I have gotten into trouble on more than one occasion because I am not a believer in Calvin's ideas of predestination, especially the teaching that, before we are born, God has already selected those who are destined for glory and those who are destined for eternal lostness. Only a few verses appear to suggest this; the majority of verses place emphasis on God's gift to us of "free will" and calling on us to make the choices that will create our futures. My take on God's directives in our lives is shaped largely by Romans 8:28. The usual translation is something like: *We know all things work together for good for those who love God, who are called according to his purpose* (NRSV). My favorite, and a more accurate translation, is given by David Bentley Hart in his 2017 translation of the New Testament: *And we know that, for those loving God, he cooperates in all ways for good with those called toward a purpose.*

> On the spiritual path there are no one-size-fits-all itineraries. [4]

Instead of following a pre-scripted agenda, I have experienced life as an unfolding, an uncovering, a series of discoveries into my personality, my gifts, and the things I love doing. This surely is the way I found my calling; I was in the right place to make those dis-

---

4   Philip Goldberg, *Roadsigns on the Spiritual Path* (Bolder, CO.: Sentient Publications, 2006), 12.

coveries because my parents were avid church goers and we lived across the street from the church: Grace Baptist Church. I even remember the pastor's name: Roy Lyons. I remember him as the kind of minister everyone would love to have: I had his ministry and the environment of grace he helped generate in this small Baptist Church. My early formative years with this congregation only affirmed that ministry was the only calling for me. Did my mother's prayer have anything to do with this? It is a question so complex that I am at a loss to supply a simple answer. I only know how things turned out – over sixty years of pastoral ministry.

HOW DOES A MINISTER LOOK?

As a young adult, I would often be asked by people I was meeting for the first time: "And what do you do?" At least one time, when replying that I was a minister, the shocked response was, "Well, you certainly don't look like a minister!"

> "You are a very odd sort of policeman."
> "I suspect that it is your idea of policemen that is odd," Grant said briskly.[5]

The above quote is from a novel by an author of another generation who continues to speak with wisdom through her writing. (More about my reading habits and recommendations in Chapter 9.) Throughout my ministry, there was always someone who would hold up to me their example of what a real minister looked like. Their model was not biblically based but was drawn from the experience of profound influence by a particular individual. If the following had been available to me during those times I would have been tempted to use it:

> You may remember the story told in Martin Buber's *Tales of the Hasidim* concerning Rabbi Zussia. Rabbi Zussia said, "At the Last Judgment, I shall not be asked, 'Why were you

---

5   Josephine Tey, *To Love and Be Wise* (New York: Scribner Paperback Fiction, 1998), 114.

not Abraham? Why were you not Moses?' I shall be asked, 'Why were you not Zussia?'" God has a vision from all eternity of the personhood of each one of us…God will ask me why I was not my own true self. That is our aim, to become truly ourselves, to realize the vision that God has of each one of us from eternity. Kallistos Ware, Bishop of Diokleia.[6]

This, of course, has nothing to do with the popular song, *I Gotta' Be Me,* which can easily be taken as the motto of the "Me Generation." Zussia was talking about being our best selves, being the unique selves that speaks to being created in the image of God. It reflects two quotes that came from somewhere and I frequently use in workshops: "Who are you going to be if you can't be yourself?" "Be yourself: Everybody else is already taken." This means tapping into individual gifts, ideals, goals, and everything that correlates with the voices within and without that speak to us of our compelling dreams and visions, that which is pulling us forward in a way that reflects who we are and what we can accomplish. It basically comes from our own hearts. "The heart is the place where we formulate our primary hopes, where we express our sense of direction, our purpose in life…At the same time…the heart is deeply ambivalent; it is a battlefield"….[7]

Future chapters will unpack this idea as I attempt to describe some of my struggles to find that real self and become the person and the minister God intended for me to become. I would like to tell you that was finally achieved, but the Conclusion of this book indicates there is still much work to be done.

NEW WAYS AND NEW PERCEPTIONS ARE NEVER EASY

It is a phrase I have heard countless times: "When God made him/her, he threw away the mold." My contention is that God

---

6 Bernadette Dieker & Jonathan Montaldo, eds., *The Prayer of the Heart* (Louisville: Fons Vitae, 2003), 10.
7 Ibid, 6.

never had any molds to begin with. Our uniqueness begins with different fingerprints and different voice prints. And it does not stop there. Uniqueness appears to be built into what it means to be created in the image of God. "That's the way it should be done" and "this is what you ought to do" were frequent pronouncements I heard throughout my ministry. All of them are based on the assumption that patterns and customs need to be perpetuated.

The role of the minister's wife in the early churches I served was modeled after the idea that it was a two for one deal. Ministry and church expectations (many unstated) were assumed to be valid for the pastor and for his wife. Throughout the early years, Sunday night services were the general rule in most Baptist churches. This was true for First Baptist Church in Rocky Mount, North Carolina. At the time, we had one son of elementary school age and another son not quite three. Sunday night services began at 7:30 p.m. By the time we made it home at night, we were lucky if we got the boys in bed by 10:00 p.m. – much too late for young children. Pat and I decided that on Sunday nights she should assume a mother's role and not the role of a pastor's wife.

Following this decision, a few Sunday nights later, at the conclusion of the service, one of the members asked me, "Where was Pat this evening?" I replied, "She's at home watching Walt Disney with the boys." She paused for a moment and then said, "Well, isn't that nice?" "Yes, it is," was my response. During the next several weeks, Pat told me that a number of parents with younger children thanked her for being a model that let them off the hook for required attendance.

Gradually, Sunday night services became a thing of the past. But not everywhere. When I came to Broadway Baptist in Louisville, despite very low attendance, Sunday night services remained on the agenda. None of the tricks of the trade could persuade the non-attenders to add it to their schedules. Attendance grew smaller, with only the die-hards present. Time came for discussion and a vote at a Deacons' meeting on whether they should continue (most of the deacons did not attend). Many ideas were presented, including this one: "I am not able to attend on Sunday nights, but it is such a good feeling to drive by the church and see the lights on." Thankfully, I was speechless. Another deacon came to my rescue with: "Well, let me make this suggestion. Why don't we install a timer on the lights so that they come on each Sunday night?" After the expected laughter, an almost unanimous vote determined that there would no longer be any Sunday night services.

Rough Beginnings

1949-1954

Blessed those who find their strength in you,
Whose hearts are set on pilgrimage. Psalm 84:4b, NJB.

SCANDAL HITS MY HOME CHURCH

When my parents moved to the West End of Louisville, attendance at Grace Baptist meant a long streetcar ride. The nearest church was Eighteenth Street Baptist Church just a few blocks away. As an older teen, I did the scouting for the family and was impressed by the pastor's sermons and the spirited singing of the choir and congregation. In a few weeks we had decided it was the church for us. At this point in my life, I do not think I had heard the term fundamentalist or had any idea what a Landmark church was all about. And so began my uncertain, uncharted, and life-changing pilgrimage. I immediately noticed that, unlike Grace Baptist, on the Sundays when we were to observe Communion, the pastor would invite all those not affiliated with Eighteenth Street to leave the service during the last hymn. The "Lord's Supper" was only for the members of the local congregation. It was "closed Communion" in its most extreme form.

For the early years, there are no adjectives large enough to describe what my association with this congregation meant to me.

Truly, I had found a church home. An added plus was the establishment of Louisville Baptist High School as a ministry. (It had nothing to do with the issue of integration in the public schools; its purpose was to provide an education in a Christian context.) As a part of the annual youth revival in the church and the Gospel Team in the high school, I was given my first opportunities in the pulpit. Gratefully, no copies of sermons preached during that period remain, but I was told I was a "live wire" in the pulpit. (I did not ask how many short-circuits occurred!)

Suddenly, all that was shattered on a Wednesday night when I entered the sanctuary for a business meeting and discovered an overflow crowd. When the meeting began, the pastor (who was the moderator) read a list of members he recommended for dismissal from membership. A vote was taken; the motion passed. Stunned was the least of my reactions. Chaos erupted with shouting and people running down the aisle to get access to the microphone. The story gradually emerged that the names on that list were persons who had signed a petition to dismiss the pastor because of unbecoming conduct, the sexual harassment of one of the girls in the senior class of the high school. Over the next several months my secure church world collapsed and my future took a new shape.

The scandal eventually reached the front pages of the local paper. I remained with the group that supported the pastor and did not believe the charges against him. Briefly, here are some of things that filled those months:

1. Several business meetings followed, with the police called in to maintain order.
2. The church became sharply divided between those who supported the pastor and those who maintained his guilt.
3. Both sides secured attorneys and a court trial followed to determine which side had valid claims to the church property.
4. I was called to testify because I had taken one of the

counts on one of the many motions that surfaced at the business meetings. All of those from the opposing side testified that I had been one of the counters on the initial Wednesday night when the pastor read his list of those he wanted stricken from the role of church membership. I had not been one of the counters for this vote and it only strengthened my belief that the charges were false.

5. The court awarded the property to those who believed the pastor was guilty of all charges. Those of us who were now literally "on the outs" formed a new congregation and began meeting in a rented facility a few miles from Eighteenth Street. I was asked to be the interim preacher until our pastor felt he could return. I was only eighteen.

6. In the meantime, the pastor continued with a Sunday afternoon live broadcast on a local radio station. He asked if I would participate by reading letters that came from listeners.

7. Early on one Sunday morning at our new rental church home, one of the members called me aside with a brief announcement: "We have evidence that the pastor is guilty of all the charges of sexual harassment."

8. That afternoon, when I arrived at the radio station, I told the pastor I would not be staying for the broadcast because I had found out the truth. He was a big man, powerfully built, and I was fortunate that he responded with silence, not violence. I left the studio and never saw him again. I resigned my position with the church and began my search for a new place of worship. Shortly thereafter, the pastor left town and the church that was being held for his return disbanded.

A NEW TIME IN A NEW PLACE

> *Why be downcast, why all these sighs?*
> *Hope in God!* Psalm 42:5, NJB.
> *Send out your light and your truth; they shall be my guide,*
> *To lead me to your holy mountain to the place where you dwell.* Psalm 43:3, NJB.

Some might call this looking for "Plan B" since "Plan A" had not worked out. I see it as the transition for a new time and place in my pilgrimage. My memories of my years at Eighteenth Street include: relationships with many wonderful people; the place where I confirmed my calling to ministry, opportunities for preaching, and, yes, getting my feet wet in church politics.

My new place was to be Virginia Avenue Baptist Church, possessing a deeply spiritually seasoned minister, a warm and welcoming congregation, and the possibility of new friendships. It was literally life changing; it was the place where I met my future wife, Pat Downard.

The years quickly rolled by with a first year at the University of Louisville and three years at Georgetown College. The richness and grace of those years is beyond description. I never doubted for a moment that I was being led by God's light and truth. For a while at least, the uneven ground had become level and the rough places had been made a plain (Isaiah 40:4, NRSV). The only negative was that, after my first year in the seminary, due to conflict between some faculty members and the president, thirteen professors were dismissed. I did not have the heart (or the necessary funds) to return the next fall. It took so long for me to resume my studies that, at one point, it seemed likely that I might be receiving my diploma and my first social security check at the same time.

Rural Enlightenments

1957-1963

*Not to us, O Lord, but to you goes all the glory
for your unfailing love and faithfulness.*
Psalm 115:1, NLT.

GETTING MY FEET WET

During my year at Southern Seminary, one of the students asked if I would be open to a "student" pastorate in a rural church not far from Louisville (this was a Sunday only commitment). I preached for several Sundays, survived the interview process, and became pastor of Old Cedar Baptist Church in Owen County.

It is difficult for me to imagine how kind and understanding the members of this small congregation must have been; almost everything I was doing was for the first time. My sermons were biblical in the sense that I read a lot of Scripture as I preached. My basic library (other than first year seminary texts) consisted of *Cruden's Complete Concordance*[8] and *The New Chain- Reference Bible*;[9] both were based on the King James translation. Seminary

---

8   Alexander Cruden, *Cruden's Complete Concordance* (Philadelphia: The John C. Winston Co., 1949).
9   Frank Charles Thompson, ed., *The New Chain-Reference Bible* (Indianapolis: B.B. Kirkbridge Bible Co., 1934).

was beginning to make me aware of the multiple complex contexts of the Bible's library of books.

When anyone proclaims, "The Bible says," I want to interrupt with: "No. This is what you are saying it says." When an expert in religious law approaches Jesus with the question, *"What must I do to receive eternal life?"* Jesus responds with: *"What does the law of Moses say? HOW do you read it?"* (Luke 10:25-26, NLT; emphasis mine). It is not what is read, but how it is interpreted that provides meaning. In a prehistorical myth, an inquirer asks a wise one: "What is holding up the earth?" "An elephant," is the wise response. "And what is holding up the elephant?" "Another elephant." The next obvious question is: "And what is holding up the second elephant?" The reply answers any further questions: "It's elephants all the way down." In reading the Bible, it is interpretation all the way down. And so began my journey of paying careful attention to what the Bible says and, most importantly, to how I am reading it. It continues to this day.

Most of my missteps were treated gently and I was met with kindness and generosity. I enjoyed Sunday dinners consisting of three salads, four meats, seven vegetables, and three desserts that were always served with the same question: "Which one do you want - first?" After viewing the same Sunday suit for several months, one family bought me a new suit from Owenton's finest men's shop. For two years I was a pastor and the third year found my wife (Pat) and me living in the parsonage. A move was on the horizon with a new set of circumstances and experiences that would give my life the new shaping it so desperately needed.

NEW OPPORTUNITIES AND LARGER CHALLENGES

Vine Run Baptist Church in Grant County had a larger congregation that was to offer three years of many unexpected blessings and challenges. The parsonage stood a short distance from the church on a high hill overlooking the valley and the small village of Folsom at the foot of the hill. Our first son was to arrive less than three months after our move. Mark spent almost four years in the warm and caring embrace of a loving congregation and several adoptive grandparents.

You would think that in this setting the problems would be few and far between. Nevertheless, with my built-in ingenuity, drive for perfection (which, of course is impossible to attain), and lack of sufficient pastoral experience, I had the creative ingenuity to mishandle enough conflict to keep things interesting. Conflict is a given in every church situation; it comes with the territory. In my early years of ministry, my goal was to avoid as much conflict as possible. In my later years, my goal was to attempt to manage conflict in a constructive and redemptive way. My big problem at Vine Run was that I had no real understanding of the kind of leadership and authority that had been established long before I arrived on the scene. The chairman of deacons (Sam) was also the individual who had literally built the parsonage and was viewed as the first person to look to when decisions needed to be made. I was big on pastoral leadership. Clashes were inevitable.

Various things shaped my time and efforts at Vine Run:

1. One semester of commuting to Louisville for seminary on Tuesday morning and returning late Friday afternoon.
2. For one semester, I taught an anatomy and physiology course at Kentucky Southern College for a class of nurses at Louisville's Baptist Hospital.
3. One year, I taught Biology at Williamsburg High School.
4. One Sunday morning, I woke up with partial facial paralysis. It was diagnosed as Bell's palsy. The doctor told me I had used up all the energy in my body (all the vitamins and minerals). My young age aided in a full recovery.

My role in the church was multiple. I mimeographed (most do not remember that messy process) the morning worship folder, led the congregational singing, and preached on Sunday morning and Sunday night. Someone came up with the idea that we needed a small electronic church organ. I introduced the idea at a deacon's meeting with the suggestion that we have a fund drive to raise the necessary $2,500 (a large sum in those days). The motion was defeated.

Someone on the Music Committee suggested that we get permission to ask certain members: "We can't do a fundraiser for the new organ. If we're able to secure one, how much would you be willing to give?" We raised the necessary funds in two weeks. Pat had played the accordion for a number of years so could read music and had a good sense of timing. She became the organist and did a commendable job (under the circumstances!). The choir practice was on Sunday night prior to the service and people began to come early just to listen. I was the director and the most that can be said for our musical efforts is that we all had a good time!

THE FRACTURE ENLARGES

One incident that I have been unable to erase from my "How could you?" memory bank occurred when we were discussing at a deacons' meeting the need for a small church office. I had suggested an area (a little larger than a closet) toward the rear of the building. Our space needs were minimum and I felt this would be a simple way to provide the space. Sam, the deacon chair, informed us that when the church was built there was space provided for a church office. When I asked the location of that space, I was told it was on the second floor over my proposed suggestion. All that was necessary was the erection of stairs. "Of course," he cautioned, "since there is no way to heat or cool the space, it is going to be awfully hot in the summer and very cold in the winter." A phrase broke loose from the inner recesses of past frustrations, and I said, "That's about the worst suggestion I have ever heard." I learned the hard way the need for a "reflective response" instead of an "emotional reaction." We got the office space I had recommended but the cost in psychological damage was high.

THE ONLY REAL REVIVAL I EVER EXPERIENCED

In August, it was common for rural churches to have a two-week revival. We compromised and had an eight-day (Sunday to Sunday) series of preaching and "special music." A good friend, Louis, came to do the preaching. He was a dynamic speaker and the sanctuary was full for almost every service. On the second Sunday morning, during the invitation hymn, Fred, one of the younger men, responded and asked if he could speak to the congregation for a moment. To a hushed assembly, he made his request. "Most of you know that my sister-in-law and I have not spoken for a year. I want you to pray for me this afternoon; I intend to go to her house and make things right." There was not a doubt in my mind that this was real revival.

However, following the service, Alice, the daughter-in-law of the deacon chair, Sam, asked if she could have a few moments of my time. We stepped to a quiet place in the sanctuary and she said, "Everyone knows that you and Sam have not had a very positive relationship. As Fred goes to talk with his sister-in-law, I think it would be the perfect time for you to go and make things right with Sam." My unspoken emotional response was, "Surely this is carrying revival too far." Pausing long enough to think, I gave a reflective response: "I think that would be a splendid idea. I will do it."

At lunch in the parsonage, I told Pat and Louis the proposal that Alice had made. Louis immediately confirmed it with: "That sounds wonderful. Pat and I will pray for you as you go to visit Sam." My response was also immediate: "Why don't you go and visit Sam and Pat and I will pray for you." They both laughed and I knew I was condemned. That afternoon I also did some praying as I drove to Sam's house; I prayed that he would not be home. But he was and, in essence, his response was: "I don't know how things got so out of kilter. It is time to make things right and I'm glad you came to see me." We agreed that during the invitation, we would meet halfway up the church aisle and both walk toward the front together.

That night when the service began, on the second row to my right I spotted Fred. He was seated between his brother and his sister-in-law. During the invitation, Sam and I met as agreed and I shared with the congregation what we had done and reminded them of the reconciled family seated on the second row. It was a glorious service and I almost hesitated to proceed with what had to be the next agenda in the service.

Pat and I had done a lot of talking and planning during the previous weeks. We knew that if I was ever to complete my seminary training, we had to move back to Louisville. So, at the conclusion of the service that night, I asked Louis to read my letter of resignation to the seated congregation. There was stunned silence as the people stood for the benediction and then came by to speak to Louis and me as we remained at the front. Pat was so emotional that she was unable to play a note of organ music. As I remember, hardly a word was spoken by anyone as they shook my hand. It was one of the few times in my life that I experienced something I can only call holy silence. It was the note on which to leave and begin the next phase of our journey.

You Never Know What Might Be Next

1964-1970

Show me the path where I should walk, O Lord;

point out the right road for me to follow.

Psalm 25:4, NLT.

BEING A PART OF THE SEMINARY'S GOLDEN YEARS

We moved to Louisville and one of the apartments in Seminary Village, only a few blocks from Southern Seminary. Across from us, opposite a common, one of my best friends and his wife moved into an apartment from which he could yell across the grassy common for immediate communication. Tom Cleveland kept me up to date on the latest James Bond movie as well as other relevant things in the culture. Our rural churches provided many things but not this kind of close association with friends of long standing. Those seminary years were filled with lots of hard work, difficult moments that dropped in without notice, and abundant good times. My weekends involved a commitment as interim Minister of Music at Virginia Avenue Baptist Church. This was not one of my better endeavors but it certainly helped pay expenses.

These were some of the seminary's golden years and I was on hand to be taught by some of the outstanding professors in the progressive years of the Southern Baptist Convention. Clyde Francisco, Eric Rust, John Carlton, and Wayne Oates were among that number. Prof Johnson was in a category by himself. He taught the only speech course offered; it was not a course in speech making but a course that focused on how to use the voice. When Prof read the Christmas story from Luke, it was like hearing it for the first time. The text came alive because the reading lifted the words from the page and brought them into a new hearing experience. The only parallel I could remember was the program at Georgetown College when Agnes Morehead came to do a night of readings. That course changed my life and my ministry.

With graduation time around the corner, the inevitable question surfaced: "Do you have any leads yet for a place to go?" I did not. I really didn't have any contacts. Tongue in cheek, I usually answered the question with: "I guess I'll just have to rely on my Scouting Angel." Deep down it really was my only contact! That Scouting Angel turned out to be the husband of one of Pat's college roommates who was working in what was termed social ministries. In one of his travels for "field work," he was asked by one of the attendees if he knew any students who were about ready to graduate from the seminary. He told him he only really knew one who was still looking for a place; he gave him my name. A contact was made. This process resulted in the call to become pastor of one of the historic Baptist churches in Richmond, Virginia: Pine Street in Oregon Hill (located within a stone's throw of the famous Hollywood Cemetery).

BLESSINGS AND CHALLENGES FOR A YOUNG PASTOR

As I look back now, it is only with affection and gratitude that I remember my five years with this congregation. Pine Street offered the ideal nurturing and training for a first full-time pastorate. None of my mistakes were fatal; some left a scar or two and, on a few occasions, a noticeable limp. Gil Kidd was the A-plus part time Minister of Music and Edlow Craig, chair of the committee that called me, was my ongoing counselor and most helpful friend. The church was warm and caring, the ideal place for our young son and a great springboard for the arrival of the second. It was a place where we felt graced and loved.

However, there are always some challenging relationships. One of these was Richard (not his name) who was prominent in church leadership. The former pastor was his idol and, in many respects, his adopted son. During that pastor's years, Richard lived only a couple of blocks from the church and the pastor would stop by two or three times a week. (When I came, he lived several miles away.) The former pastor left to become pastor of one of the largest and most prominent Baptist churches in Virginia. In Richard's eyes, walking on water came second nature to his never to be equaled model of the perfect pastor. Plus, his pulpit abilities were second to none. It was almost like being the next speaker after the Apostle Paul had finished his presentation. It was no contest and I would have been wise not to have made it one; it was unwinnable, but because ministers as a group want to be loved and accepted, I thought I would at least give it a try.

I should have applied the wisdom of the old 80/10/10 rule someone had passed my way: When you come to a new congregation, ten percent of the people will think you are the best pastor they have ever had; eighty percent will affirm your ministry and participate if they feel you like them and are working at your job; ten percent will wonder where the committee got your name. The advice was to concentrate on the eighty percent in the middle, express gratitude for the ten percent at the top, and pray for the strength to deal graciously with the ten percent at the bottom; you will never win them over. I was convinced I could make Richard the exception.

Richard, a fire chief, continued to sit each Sunday, dressed in his uniform, to my left on the front row. During the service, his ear phone kept him plugged into a special service sending current fire call information. The distant look and the tilted head signaled an alert for somewhere in the city. None ever involved him personally but he continued to remain fire chief in residence; he certainly was not a fire chief listening to my sermon. There never was a reconciling service like the one at Vine Run; I managed to cooperate with the inevitable, and attempted to keep my focus on those who were plugged into the service and the sermon.

My basic seminary education and even graduate study offered only a one-semester course in pastoral care. Most dealt with theology and homiletics (preaching); most of my difficulties were people centered. Conferences and extensive reading finally brought a little light to this darkened corner of my education. My hindsight response to Richard would have been one based primarily on listening; there would have been no place in it for a confrontational approach. I probably would have begun with something like: "I have heard many good things about your former minister. Tell me the things that made him such an outstanding pastor. What do you miss most now that he is gone?" My efforts would have gone into doing what I could to be pastor on whatever level he would make possible. I would never have been his ministerial cup of tea.

One of the snapshots that has pasted itself in my book of memories is that of Sarah (not her real name, although, over fifty years later, I do remember the first and last name) who was our self-appointed church critic. Nothing was ever quite right in the life of the church and she kept careful notes on each shortcoming. On this day, her complaint had to do with the lack of information being received by the congregation. Despite a monthly newsletter, written and verbal announcements during Sunday morning worship, and announcement sheets distributed to every Sunday School department leader, she felt we were not getting the job done.

Our next big event was the Budget Fair coming in a little over a month. There were booths and displays of the various ministries and missions of the church with notations of the necessary funding required. There was also the addition of the Minister of Music's production of *The Grasshopper Opera* (a piece unknown to lovers of fine music). I put the information wheels into high gear. The newsletter featured the event. Announcements were made each Sunday morning with complete information printed in the worship folder. On the Sunday morning before the event that night, I personally attached an announcement sheet to the door of every Sunday School class. The Budget Fair had overflow attendance and everyone commented on the huge success of everything, especially the comic opera. I went to sleep that night with one thought running through my head: Mission Accomplished!

The following Sunday morning, shortly before worship, Sarah found me with an observation: "I heard you had a great crowd last Sunday night at the Budget Fair." "Yes," I responded, "it was more than we had hoped for." She gave me a stern look and said, "Well, I just want you to know that, if I had known anything about it, I would have attended." Wisdom prevailed and I made no comment. In a moment, she walked away with her usual confidence: Mission Accomplished! One of my toughest lessons was to stay off the defensive. Once you assume that position, you are on the losing end of the conversation. With critics, you simply receive their information with all the courtesy and grace you can muster and thank them for their continuing interest in the life and ministry of the church. They are not "fixable."

THEOLOGY 101

Wednesday nights meant an on-going Bible study. It provided the opportunity for more than the monologue of Sunday preaching. On many occasions, it was obvious that I was learning more than they were. For example: I pointed out that In the Old Testament we read much about God seeing, hearing, and speaking (and even smelling). The analogy ended with: "Nobody believes God has a face like humans, with eyes, ears, mouth, and a nose." Immediately, a voice from the back of the room boomed out, "I do!" At first, I thought it was meant to be humorous, but I soon discovered his reading of Scripture was quite literal. A lengthy discussion followed about the "pictures" of God given to us in the Hebrew Scriptures.

Somewhat later, in a series on the Gospel of John, we came to chapter three with the account of Jesus turning water into wine. I had hardly gotten into the context and content of the story when a woman spoke up: "We all know that wasn't really wine; it was Welchade." As I groped for an appropriate pastoral response, another woman spoke up: "No, that cannot be right. Those present said it was the best wine that had yet been served at the wedding feast. I believe that Jesus turned that water into wine, but I confess: it has been an embarrassment to me all my life!" It would have been a real embarrassment if she had known that, according to the text, Jesus made between one hundred twenty and one hundred fifty gallons of wine! That for people who had already been drinking for a considerable amount of time.

A REAL MISSTEP

Although Pine Street had a relatively large congregation, it had many of the characteristics of a family church. Some of the key families had played major roles in the history of the church. My church secretary was a part of one of those families. She was an excellent secretary with knowledge of the membership that was very helpful in visitation. All went well for over four years. Into my fifth year, in a personnel meeting where we talked about ways of improving the work of the staff, I made a casual (and totally uncalled for!) observation: "If my secretary could stay off the phone a little, she could probably get some other things done." A member of the committee was a member of that family and she conveyed my remark to the secretary who immediately resigned. A strained relationship marked the rest of my last year and nothing I did could repair the hurt feelings. One of the rules of a happy marriage is the same for a happy staff: every day leave one or two things unsaid. Being true doesn't mean it has to be spoken. To this day, I do not think I have ever fully forgiven myself for this transgression.

The years brought the regular church disagreements and conflicts but none as traumatic as this one. A search committee from another church began visiting our services which ultimately resulted in my moving to North Carolina. Five years seemed like an appropriate time and most of the congregation appeared very satisfied with what had been accomplished and where they were as a congregation. I left with their blessings and good wishes for my next place of ministry.

A Little Rocky in Rocky Mount

1970-1974

*Direct me in your ways…
And teach me your paths.* Psalm 25:4, NJB.

First Baptist Church in Rocky Mount, North Carolina, was to be the largest church of my pastorates and the most southern in culture. There were many "dear hearts and gentle people" (right out of Doris Day's popular hit recording). We were welcomed as the young pastor and his family who were going to be the springboard for younger families joining the congregation. It always seemed to be the "numbers game" that spelled success or failure in church life. It was a confession of identity when the Southern Baptist Convention adopted as one of its themes, "A Million More in Fifty-Four." I mentioned to one of my fellow pastors, I sometimes feared that with the primary aim set on growth, we might one day discover our theme to be, "Up a Tree in Sixty-Three." It took a little longer than that but the tree already seemed to be taking root.

With the coming of any new pastor, there is usually a period of increased church attendance due, if nothing more, than the novelty of a new voice in the pulpit. Sometimes the growth has a little different color than expectations had in mind. First, I need to set the stage for what proved to be the most traumatic "situation" in my four years at First Baptist.

The first days on our new "church field" were filled with exciting possibilities and opportunities and new friends to enrich our lives in ways we had not before experienced. The first months seemed to overflow with extended helping hands assisting us in making a home in Rocky Mount.

Two early episodes made those helping hands necessary hands. The week before we were to move from Richmond to Rocky Mount, I was at the church for a full week getting things organized and ready for our move. The day I was ready to drive back to Richmond, Pat called with the news that she had gone roller skating with some of the young people from the church and had fallen and broken her right wrist. I hope I was speechless when she told me because I have yet to have a helpful positive response.

We made the move and somehow got everything in place and had sufficient help until the cast was removed. Just in time however for the second event. It was a few minutes before eleven and I was preparing to enter the sanctuary for a funeral service that was to begin at eleven o'clock. My secretary opened the door of my office to announce, "Your wife is on the phone and she says it is an emergency." I answered the phone with, "What's wrong?" and heard an almost tearful voice lament: "It's awful. I was in the attic looking for something in one of the boxes and did not notice where I was stepping. I missed the beam and my foot went all the way through the drywall a little beyond my knee. It took me forever to get out and get down here to the telephone. (This was before cell phones were in common usage). Although I recall my first words as, "Are you all right?", she maintains my first words were, "Is there a lot of damage to the ceiling?" I was a few minutes late for the funeral service but had enough time to ascertain she was a little shaken up but reasonably okay. She was going to call a neighbor to be with her until I could get home after the service. Thus ended the crisis.

Everywhere we looked it appeared life was full of promises in this small city only a few miles from the state capitol of Raleigh. There began to appear, however, a few disturbing signs, one more literal than the others. I found myself one Saturday on the road to nearby Wilson to obtain something we needed for our new house. It was all I could do to keep the car on the road when I saw to my right, looming large and threatening, a huge billboard with the bold letters: "Welcome to Klan Country."

I knew this sign did not speak for most of the members of my congregation but it did alert me to an element in the culture that would not go unnoticed. It surfaced early in a seemingly unlikely place. I became a member of the Ministerial Association which was composed of the major churches and denominations (including the Pentecostal) in the city. There was also another organization consisting of churches we would call "fundamentalist," always on guard defending the basics of the Christian faith (as they saw and interpreted them). That group had written a letter to the state education department protesting the use of one of the textbooks in the local schools. They complained it contained the phrase "that damn cat" which was language they did not want to see in a book their children were reading. It also contained a very large picture of Martin Luther King, Jr. which, I am also certain they did not want them to see. They requested that the book be removed immediately.

The ministerial association of which I was a member, countered with the plea that a local group not be permitted to censor which books were used as texts in our local schools. This, we contended, should be left to the state organization which was always open to parental concerns. The problem was, on a Sunday morning, this story appeared in large print on the front page of the local morning newspaper, including the names of all the pastors who were members of each group. I was in the sanctuary following the early Sunday morning service when one of the members came charging down a church aisle, almost shouting as she arrived at the front, "I can't believe my pastor endorses cursing." I immediately responded, "The issue has nothing to do with cursing. I'm just not a member of the John Birch Society." Her immediate response was, "Well, I am!"

I had many unspoken rules to live by in the pastorate but found them easily violated without any advance notice. An emotional reaction to any question or situation was never the best response; it was almost always regretted. What I should have given that day was a "reflective response" which always calls for time to do that reflecting. Nothing about my comment was either wise or pastoral. A member of my congregation was genuinely upset over the newspaper article and I needed to attempt to understand her concern and calmly talk about the reason for the stance of the ministerial group to which I belonged. Once again, a confrontational response from a defensive position is never helpful. It took many weeks and several sessions to begin to repair the damage of my attack on the John Birch Society. (Only a few members of the congregation belonged to the organization). The entire situation should have alerted me to some of the underlying fear and anxiety in parts of the culture. The issues raised by the Civil War were far from over.

Perhaps that prepared me for an announcement that came shortly later in one of the deacons' meetings. Following his opening prayer, the chairman had hardly called the meeting to order when one deacon stood and announced, "I have a major concern which needs to be addressed immediately." He was given the floor and the attention of the remaining forty deacons (all men, of course). "Most of you are aware that Frances, a black woman (not her real name but I remember all of it well), has been attending our services. She has told a couple of the deacons, now that the new pastor has come, she is ready to join the church." I looked to make certain no one was about to suffer heart failure but the silence and the wide eyes conveyed the anxiety being experienced.

After a period of extended silence, one of the deacon's spoke up: "Well, I've heard she is being paid $30 a week to attend our church." I happened to already know this deacon by name and reputation and responded in a matter-of-fact way, "Oh, Harry, I wouldn't let that out. A lot of people I know would love to get in on that!" No one inquired as to the source of the information Harry and I provided but they did wait for the chairman to propose a course of action. After much discussion, it was decided that one of the deacons and I would make a home visit to Frances and find out why she wanted to join First Baptist. The deacon selected to accompany me was Philip, one of the older men and a true saint of God if ever there was one. I could not have made a better selection. We arranged for a visit to be made before the next deacons' meeting.

The first order of business at the next meeting was our report and Philip stood to address the group in his calm, slow, southern manner. The conclusion: Philip and I saw no reason why Frances should not be received as a member. Much discussion followed, resulting in approval by the deacons. Philip called to inform her of our decision. All we had to do was wait for the Sunday she decided to join. For a couple of Sundays, I was so anxious that I think I remember praying that no one would come forward during the invitation hymn. On the following Sunday, during the first stanza of the last hymn, Frances, with hand extended, made her way down the aisle to meet me at the front. I greeted her as I did all who came forward but did notice that to my right on the second row, three older women put their hands over their hearts and fell back into the pew. My first thought was: well, this is the end of my brief tenure at First Baptist. No, not yet. One of the most amazing responses to the invitation was about to occur. On the second stanza, a husband and wife and their two small children came forward for transfer of membership. I had never seen them before. On the third stanza, a young couple came forward for membership. I had never seen them before. On the fourth stanza, a couple and their two teenage children came forward to join. I had never seen them before. The congregation was literally awestruck to see eleven people seated on the front pew waiting to be received into the fellowship of the church.

The hymn concluded; I asked the congregation to be seated and I proceeded to introduce Frances with the usual routine for the acceptance of new members. This concluded, I was about to move to the first couple, when suddenly, from my left, a voice boomed from the last row under the balcony: "I rise to a point of order. I move that a called business meeting be held to deal with the matter of this membership." Since ignorance can be one of my long suits, I responded, "I'm sorry but I don't understand. We have received Frances just like we do all who come for membership." Before I could think of something else to say, from my right only a few pews from me, the chairman of deacons unwound his long frame and, reminding me of Gregory Peck in *To Kill a Mockingbird*, announced calmly, "I'm sorry, Mr. Todd. I'm going to have to rule you out of order and ask you to be seated." He was seated. The service proceeded. Following the benediction, the new members remained at the front and the congregation filed by to extend what Baptists call "the right hand of Christian fellowship." Believe it or not, I never heard another word about any problem concerning the membership of an African American at First Baptist.

TROUBLE AT TIMES SEEMED TO BE MY MIDDLE NAME

Being a cooperating Baptist meant being a part of the local association. Well into my third year in Rocky Mount, I attended the annual associational meeting. The pastor of Lakeside Baptist Church had become one of my best friends; his church was known as the liberal Baptist church in town. A motion was introduced by one of the more conservative pastors that Lakeside be "disfellowshipped" (a term Baptist love because it sounds better than "kicked out") from the association. Their transgression? They were receiving members from other denominations without rebaptism. Most Baptists did not believe that baptism was necessary for salvation but, evidently, it was necessary to be baptized by an "authorized" church.

Sidebar: Some felt the tag "authorized" belonged only to Baptist churches. Early in my ministry I was given a copy of

"The Trail of Blood" which traced the Baptist church all the way back to John the Baptist, proving it was the only true church.

The term "alien immersion" was used at the meeting. The term refers to being baptized by someone outside the Baptist church, therefore, not authorized baptism. For those with any kind of an ecumenical spirit, it didn't make sense. When the vote by a show of hands was taken, I was one who voted not to exclude Lakeside from the association. The motion was defeated but those who voted against the motion were numbered among the liberals (whatever that term meant). There were a few raised eyebrows in my congregation, but the issue quickly faded away. Trouble was never far off from those of us who had a different makeup to our faith. I was increasingly developing a faith that was firm at the center and flexible at the edges. That center included: the Incarnation, Crucifixion, and Resurrection of Jesus; the Hebrew God of Scripture - the God of Creation, Covenant, Redemption and Consummation- the God who revealed Himself as Father, Son, and Spirit.

As I moved further to the fringes of faith, I did not feel it was necessary to have everything nailed down. Much could still be open and "awaiting further light" as our Quaker friends like to say. When I was ordained to ministry, my local church gave me a copy of a Scofield Bible. It is the King James version with a column down the center of each page in the Bible. Next to Genesis 1:1, which literally reads in the Hebrew: *When God began to create the heaven and the earth...,*[10] the Scofield Bible has this commentary: "B.C. 4004." That date comes from Archbishop Ussher who, in the 17th century, from a literal reading of Genesis, developed his chronology which some still use to defend the "young earth theory" of creation. The danger of the Scofield Bible is that too many accept the commentary as just as inspired as the text. The text says nothing about the when or how of creation, it only contends that God is the creator. That is basic. The how and when are on the

10 Robert Alter, *The Hebrew Bible* (New York: W. W. Norton, 2019).

fringes of faith. As the years increase, the center of my faith continues without question, but the margins continue to have more flexibility. I refer to them as the growing edges of my faith. If that spells trouble, I believe it is the right kind of trouble to have regarding faith. It makes conversation and dialogue with those who differ in matters of faith both possible and profitable.

At some point during these years, I took my vacation time to complete my graduate work at Southeastern Seminary outside of Raleigh. As always, this seminary opened new windows and provided fresh insights for biblical thinking and pastoral ministry. It was an unexpected blessing of my Rocky Mount years and within four years I had earned my Doctor of Ministry degree.

AND A LOT OF OTHER LITTLE THINGS ALONG THE WAY

One of the things I encountered at Rocky Mount for the first time was the Men's Bible Class which had over a hundred in regular attendance. This was a fixture in many larger churches in the south. In reality, it was another church with its own treasurer, weekly offerings, mission projects, and curriculum of their choosing. I was never able to establish much of a relationship with them but they never presented any real problem in the life of the church. They simply wanted to be left alone to do their own thing. We left them alone and they did it.

In my office one day, going through the mail, I received a four-page, handwritten letter, pouring out a litany of complaints and unhappiness about so many things in the church. Of course, it was unsigned. The treasurer of the church was not a member of First Baptist and I had come to appreciate her hard work and to trust her with many confidential matters. I floated to her the idea of checking the pledge cards to see if she could match the handwriting in the letter with any signature on the cards. As strange as it sounds, this proved to be very redemptive. A match was found and the secretary gave me a brief history of the woman writer and her family. The next Sunday morning, I recognized her on my left, seated on the fifth row. I said a silent prayer for her as I reflected on her story. She had several siblings who lived in other parts of the country. When the mother began to need special care in order to stay in her home, the family negotiated with this sister to supply the necessary funding for her to remain in the home and take care of the mother. This had continued for a number of years. She never married and her life consisted of being a caregiver. The secretary had told me she never seemed to be a very happy person. Of course not! How could she be when her life and its possibilities had been taken from her. I never confronted her about the letter. I just made certain her mother was on my list of homebound members to visit.

This episode is inserted to illustrate one of the most important things I learned as a pastor: every person has a story and you never know or understand anything about another person until you begin to know and understand their story. Judgments become fewer and less important and acceptance becomes more central as we get to know the context of the words and behavior of someone. John Carlton, my favorite homiletics professor, said something on the first day of class that went into my notes and became something I never wanted to forget (although sometimes it faded a little into the background). Dr. Carlton spoke without notes as he said, "When you stand in the pulpit on Sunday morning and look out at your congregation, never forget that everyone seated before you has some kind of trouble, some kind of burden, some kind of pain, some kind of issue that has colored their perspective, some kind of battle they are fighting, and some kind of hope they are looking for. The basic question for you, even if it is never spoken, is: 'What kind of good news do you have for me today?'" As the years went by that is why most of my sermons spoke loudly of grace, forgiveness, reconciliation, and the always available opportunity to get up and give it another try. Some might call that simply developing "a pastor's heart." It is that but I believe it is also attempting to deal with people today the way Jesus dealt with people in his day.

A final brief piece illustrates that sometimes a pastor can be caught off guard on a "I can't handle one more thing" day. The Sunday School at First Baptist was large and blessed with many excellent leaders and teachers. It was one of the major strengths and drawing cards of the church. The director of the Sunday School appeared to have dedicated his life to being that director. This was confirmed on a Sunday morning when, as his wife was leaving the service, she leaned over to whisper in my ear: "Could you please persuade my husband to stay home some nights with me and the children? He seems always to be involved in some Sunday School meeting. I would be so grateful for any help you can give." I wasn't quite sure how to deal with that request; from what I knew about her husband, I knew that much thought and careful handling would be necessary. Shortly thereafter on one of those "I need a break" days, my secretary informed me that the Sunday School director wanted to see me. I welcomed him along with his assistant director. Without any introductory remarks, his initial comment to me was: "Frank and I are both disappointed that you don't support the Sunday School." My defensive response is forgotten but not what occurred for the only time in my life: I hyperventilated! I didn't have a paper bag handy, but I gradually regained my normal breathing and continued in the conversation attempting to discover what he expected, and what it would look like if I supported the Sunday School. I never mentioned the request from his wife. I knew this was some deep water and I didn't have any scuba diving equipment available. I don't know what I promised but he and his assistant left knowing they had done their duty.

SAVING THE BEST UNTIL LAST

The biggest blessing of all, and one that would be with me for the remainder of my ministry, was my meeting Roger and Jennie Lamb. Roger was the Minister of Music and Jennie was the organist. Never had I heard the organ played the way Jennie did and never had I heard such glorious (the only appropriate word) singing by a choir. I knew I had met the best of the best. We not only worked together but became the best of friends. Sometimes the pulpit and the music ministry are in conflict; we found ourselves in perfect harmony. The Lambs worked with me in the two other churches I would serve before retirement. A few accused me of planning in advance to always "take Roger with me" but in both situations a needed change was evident to anyone who had an ear to listen.

Blue Ridge Oasis

1974-1980

*By tranquil streams he leads me
to restore my spirit.* Psalm 23:3, NJB.

THEY KEPT SHOWING UP

One Sunday I noticed some visitors in the congregation. Those of us in ministry somehow have a built-in search committee detector; I had no idea what church they represented. The only thing I knew was that I had not been at my present church long enough to think about a move. In the weeks that followed, I learned that the committee was from the First Baptist Church in Waynesboro, Virginia; it was in the heart of the Blue Ridge. Our time spent in Richmond made us familiar with the area that was only twenty-five miles north of Charlottesville, the home of Mr. Jefferson's University. At the insistence of the committee, there were some initial conversations but there was nothing that made me feel it was time to make a move.

Several months passed and, thankfully, life was uneventful in Rocky Mount. A neighboring pastor asked if I would do a weekend of preaching at his church and I accepted the invitation. There were visitors in the congregation that Sunday; one of the deacons welcomed them and knew a search committee when he saw one. They confessed their identity and he told them: "If you're looking for a new pastor, the person you need to look at is our guest speaker for this weekend, Ron Higdon." (He did not want to lose his pastor!) The committee remained for the service and later greeted me as old friends; they were the committee from First Baptist in Waynesboro. This time, I felt a strange pulling in the direction of this new situation and I could not shake it. Thus began a series of conversations.

A few weeks later, my wife and I left for a weekend visit and my "trial sermon." (This designation has hung over the initial meeting with a congregation for generations even though it poorly describes such an experience. It is a trial in the sense of the time to determine if one is a good fit for the congregation.) Following that weekend, the die was cast and in a few months we were on our way to the valley of Virginia. Some at Rocky Mount were glad to see me go, but the majority expressed gratitude for my ministry and noted they had been blessed by my being with them. I immediately let them know that the blessing was mutual. My life and ministry had indeed been blessed by my years with this congregation where I encountered some of the best people I have ever known. Despite some "rockiness," more than a few tears were shed over the loss of relationships that had enriched our lives and my ministry.

WHEREVER WE GO, THERE WE ARE

Our six years in Waynesboro were literally like an oasis following almost a decade of pastoral ministry. However, to this oasis I brought what I had taken with me to every church before: my humanity. Of the books I have written, I received more negative comments on one simply because of its subtitle: *Halo and Hoverboard Not Required: How to Develop a Fully Human Spirituality.* Most of the complaints hit the same note: "How can you combine spirituality with being fully human?" My rebuttal was: Where did we ever get the idea that they could be separated? Much of the blame goes to a misreading of Romans 7 where Paul discusses his struggle in verses 14 and 24: *We are well aware that the Law is spiritual: but I am a creature of flesh and blood sold as a slave to sin.... Who will rescue me* from *this body doomed to death?* (NJB)

As always, to understand the God given humanity which is ours, it is necessary to listen to the totality of the biblical witness. In Genesis 2, God creates the first humans, breathes his breath into them, resulting in human beings with a unity of body and spirit. The idea of a division between body and spirit is a Greek concept, not a Hebrew one. In Jesus' day those who believed in resurrection believed in a bodily resurrection. When Jesus was resurrected it was a bodily resurrection. In 1 Corinthians 15, Paul devotes an entire section of his letter to the subject of "The Resurrection Body." As one of my professors liked to say, "It is not so much that we have a soul as it is that we are a soul." Being spiritual has nothing to do with wearing a halo (living such a life of goodness that you are raised above the common lot of mortals) or riding a hoverboard and floating just a little above the cares, realities, and pitfalls of life. We are embodied spirits, embodied souls, attempting to live the spiritual life as described in the Sermon on the Mount (Matthew 5 through 7) and I Corinthians 13 (describing how we are to love our neighbors as ourselves).

I was always a fully human minister and my spirituality was always fully human. Which meant that perfection was never on the agenda but forgiveness and beginning again were always kept close at hand. What unites us is not our giftedness and our achievements but the common thread that has always made us able to understand one another: our common humanity. In the past, I often heard the lament, "What we need to do is get back to the New Testament church!" My rejoinder was: "I hope it is not the church at Corinth! I would be so embarrassed if someone got drunk on communion wine!" (one of the minor sins in this congregation located in what could easily be called the "Sin City" of its day). When Paul designates all believers as "saints," he does so with all their fully humanness in full display.

Perhaps it was the mountain air or the prevalent spirit of openness and acceptance that made it easier to largely avoid a defensive position on issues. (I think the presence of GE and Dupont in this small city contributed to this flexibility). There are always things to deal with whenever a group of people gather for any purpose; it's no different in the church. Even Paul's beloved church at Philippi had its problems. In his writing to this church, you can feel the love and affirmation at the very beginning of his letter: *"I thank my God whenever I think of you, and every time I pray for you all, I always pray with joy…NJB."* This has nothing to do with a church that has learned how to live above its full humanity. Before he ends his letter, in 4:2 he finds it necessary to say: *"I urge Euodia, and I urge Syntyche to come to agreement with each other in the Lord…NJB."* He spares us the details of this conflict but lets us know he is not addressing a perfect, other worldly, church. You do not have to be in the church world for very long to understand why the New Testament makes so much space for grace, forgiveness, and reconciliation.

RED FLAGS IN A CLOUDLESS SKY

My first week in Waynesboro brought my first challenge. The church provided a car for the pastor's use and the Minister of Music had been using it during the interim to do pastoral visitation. I had already had initial meetings with the staff and we had the usual get acquainted time. Nothing had prepared me for his entering the office on that Monday morning, throwing the keys to the car on my desk and announcing, "The church doesn't need to own a car." His abruptness spoke of deeper issues that did not involve a set of car keys. (Note: the church car died about a week later and the usual donor declined to replace it. From that point forward, as I had always done, I used my own car). I had already heard some rumblings of discontent from some members of the choir about his methods of directing. Later that week I got some specifics. "He tells us we have got to do better; we have got to put ourselves into what we are singing. We have to do it with gusto. But he never gives us any specifics as to how we can accomplish this."

As the first few weeks unfolded, some things became apparent. The Minister of Music really wanted to be a pastor. (He had probably set his sights on the position I now held). He lacked both the skills and the motivation for his present position. He seemed to be spending a lot of his time on the road and I asked him specifically why he needed to spend so much time visiting when I was now doing the pastoral visitation. He brought in a stack of receipts from his gas purchases as proof he spent a lot of time visiting. As I had been taught, I kept a daily journal in which I recorded the names of all persons I visited as well as any meetings or church related luncheons I attended. For each of these items, I recorded the odometer reading before and after each event. (I had been told that in an audit the IRS would want such proof for mileage claimed in my work). When I asked him for such a journal, he said he didn't keep one. The situation kept deteriorating. There were more complaints from choir members. His solution for any difficulty with an anthem was the cheerleaders' theme I have seen displayed at every football game I have ever attended: "Get louder."

The chairman of deacons and I had several meetings with Frank (not his real name) and offered our help in finding him a position. He found a place, made a move, and from all reports did a good job as preacher and pastor. The process was not as simple or easy as it sounds but was one of those initial necessary moves that was strategic to the life of the church and my ministry as the new pastor. A search committee was formed, I gave them Roger's name, and after exploring all the possibilities, returned to it for their first interview process. The result was that Roger became the Minister of Music and Jennie became the organist. The choir grew in numbers, the music became one of the drawing cards for the morning service, and I had someone who became part of the First Baptist team.

FOR SOME, THIS SECTION MAY BE UNSETTLING

Opening the door to the exit of the Minister of Music was neither a simple or easy accomplishment. I learned through fifteen years of ministry that one of the keys to satisfaction and accomplishment was the association with competent and cooperative people in all the areas of leadership. John Adams learned that the hard way when he basically kept Washington's cabinet instead of assembling his own. Of course, I can't imagine what it would be like to follow probably the greatest hero this country has even had. Although, I think I got a little taste of it from my experience at Pine Street when I followed a truly outstanding preacher and pastor. In making staff changes, it takes consultation, conversation, much deliberation, and tons of courage to follow Davy Crockett's advice: "Be sure you're right and then go ahead."

It has been my experience that most people had little understanding of what the life of a pastor was like. (I think that today there have been many positive changes in perspectives and provisions.) Most churches expected pastors to be married and have a family but didn't really provide much time in a schedule for being with them. The usual pattern was one day off a week, hardly enough time to catch your breath and a disturbing number when many in the congregation often took long weekends with families for travel and relaxation. There was no time clock to be punched because once you accepted the call to a church, you were pastor 24/7. "I'll not be at the committee meeting tonight because my son will be playing in a very important game," would never be a legitimate excuse for an absence. Calls for a crisis visit often came after a full day of work and before a time for a family activity. Nothing could take priority over a request someone deemed only the pastor could fulfill.

In Rocky Mount, the official homebound list numbered well over a hundred. My policy was to visit homebound members upon request, everyone who was in the hospital, everyone who experienced a loss in their family, and anyone who called asking for a visit. This was in addition to calling on persons who visited the church on Sunday and wished to talk about membership. The day of a pastor "dropping in" on members for a quick visit was long gone. If you were in a church of any size, you were never able to make all the calls some people thought you ought to be making. In one church, I received a call from a "concerned member" who informed me that two members of the congregation needed me to look in on them. I asked, "Is there some sort of problem?" "No," was the reply. "I think they just need some attention." For any visit I ever made to be effective, I had to know the purpose for my visit and there were enough of those to keep my schedule full.

Another struggle in pastoral ministry is giving oneself enough time for sermon and Bible study presentations. That included every Sunday (except for vacation time) for a sermon and every Wednesday night (except for a brief summer break) for a Bible study. Most years I preached at least forty-five sermons and did almost as many Bible studies. I did almost all these preparations at home which offered fewer interruptions and I had access to my library. My usual schedule was to begin my work each morning at five o'clock and arrive at the office about ten o'clock. I saw my biggest responsibility to make certain that I had a worthy offering on Sunday morning and that people left the service with something to take with them. It was my number one priority because it was the time for ministering to the largest number of people. I cared enough to try to give them my very best every Sunday (apologies to Hallmark). My confession at this point is that I loved what I did and working on sermons and doing ongoing Bible study was the joy of my ministry.

MEANWHILE, BACK AT WAYNESBORO

Years later, several would tell me that my six years were some of the golden years in the life of the church but not simply because I was there. The music alone was worth attending the service. One Sunday morning, following an indescribable anthem by the choir,

I stood to begin my sermon, paused, and said, "After that, we probably don't even need a sermon." It was the only time I ever said that because I got a big "Amen!" from someone in the congregation, followed by laughter. Some of the other reasons for the years being golden were: they were years when people felt church was an important part of their lives, GE and Dupont were stimulating parts of the city's life, and the church did not suffer from any major conflicts. Also, I felt that I was finally beginning to get a handle on the structure and presentation of my sermons (after about fifteen years of practice!). The big plus was that the congregation was filled with so many gifted and committed people, people who were not out of sorts with anybody or the world at large, and did not bring assorted grievances and battles with them to fight on Sunday morning. I will add what sounds too simplistic but is true: simply just good people!

There were many memorable people in that congregation. Two I vividly recall with gratitude and great affection. They were both widows in their eighties. One called me on several occasions and said, "Stop by the house because I have just baked some Sally Lunn bread for you." This bread is one of the classic Williamsburg traditions and there is just nothing like it; she knew how to do it to perfection. Anna and her friend Lucille were present at almost every celebration I ever attended. Once, I was standing behind them in a reception line and overheard a remarkable conversation. Anna asked: "How are you?" Lucille responded, "Deteriorating gradually, how are you?" "Oh, I think I'm okay but I have these friends who call me every morning to see if I'm dead." "Have you ever been?" "No, but once, I thought I was. But I wasn't." Neither had anything about them that spoke of deadness. They illustrated the famous quote that comes from St. Irenaeus: "The glory of God is a human being fully alive." In spite of hardships, difficulties, and losses they never stopped the business of being fully alive.

Of course, there were the usual bumps and grinds that are a part of any healthy relationship but really no traumatic events. It seemed as though this would continue, until my wife's sister gave her boss a tape of one of the sermons I had preached. He was a member of Broadway Baptist Church in Louisville and he passed this tape to the chair of the Pastor Search Committee.

AN OPPORTUNITY LOADED WITH RISKS

Even in the initial conversations with some of the search committee, I learned enough to be aware of some built-in risks in this situation. The pastor who just retired had been with the congregation for thirty years. He was much loved and respected as a pastor and noted as one of the community's outstanding leaders. He had weathered the storm of shepherding the church in its move from inner-city Louisville to the rapidly growing east end of the city. The phrase that kept running through my mind was one I had heard many times: "A thirty-year pastorate is followed by a two-year pastorate which is followed by a thirty-year pastorate." The patterns, traditions, methods, and simply the ways of doing just about everything are well set over such a long period of time; many would have to be reviewed and revised for life and ministry to be relevant in the present. My first reaction to the situation was not very positive.

That changed with the visit from Louisville of two members of the committee and luncheon at the Boar's Head Inn in Charlottesville. (It, and the University of Virginia, were only twenty-five miles from Waynesboro. Close by was Jefferson's historic Monticello. History just leaped out at you everywhere you turned. It was an enriching place to live). Even though my wife and I were from Louisville, our two visitors gave us some new perspectives. Broadway was located near the Southern Baptist Theological Seminary and the church boasted a rather large number of professors as members and Sunday School teachers. Who knows? I might even be given the opportunity to do some teaching there. The associations and friendships I could make would provide an educational experience no book or degree had offered.

As they described the openness and flexibility of the congregation, they presented the picture of a congregation ready for change and growth (emphasis on the growth!). They were both persons you would want to get to know better and they assured us that there was no preconceived model of a pastor and his wife into which we had to fit. In fact, we could even dance together at wedding receptions. Over the next several weeks there were many conversations and we finally found ourselves ready to journey to Louisville for a weekend get acquainted visit with a "trial" sermon on Sunday. Little did we suspect that we were getting ready to commit our lives for the next twenty years.

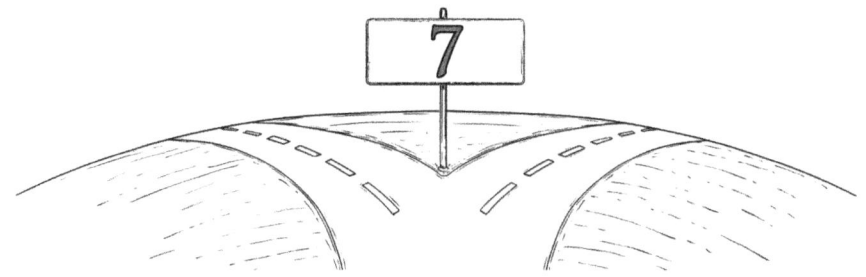

A Wider World of Opportunity and Crisis

1980-2001

*How much you have done,
Yahweh, my God –
Your wonders, your plans for us –
You have no equal!* Psalm 40:5, NJB.

I continue to be overwhelmed as I look back on the twenty years at Broadway and consider the exceedingly large number of kind and generous people who dominated its history. My personal response to those years is once again summarized in Paul's heartfelt love and appreciation for the church at Philippi: *I thank my God whenever I think of you, and every time I pray for you all, I always pray with joy for your partnership in the gospel from the very first day up to the present* (1:3-5, NJB). I was about to step into a much wider world that was shortly to include the battle for the institutions of the Southern Baptist Convention. Southern Seminary was one of those institutions on the takeover agenda.

The church staff with its weekly meetings has always been at the center of my concept of leadership. These meetings provide the opportunity for bringing all of us up to date on the various ministries of the church and general reports on how the other ministers felt things were going. When I came to Broadway, my staff consisted of an extremely gifted and effective Minister of Education, a full-time organist, and a part-time Minister of Music. As I remember it, volunteers took care of children and youth ministries. Without the participation of a full-time Minister of Music there was a huge gap in the needed voices at the table. I attempted to make my case for the position to be full-time.

To complicate matters further, the Minister of Music was on a full year's sabbatical from his seminary position. When the decision was finally made to make the music position full-time, it was first offered to the current Minister of Music who only wanted a part-time position. A search committee was formed and, of course, I gave them Roger Lamb's name as one to consider. There were quite a few unhappy campers over the departure of a truly loved choir director. However, the restructuring of the staff was not unlike a president getting the right mix in his cabinet. Some of the conflict swirled around the issue of exactly who was going to be in charge. Disrupting long standing patterns and methods is never easy because it involves the most difficult word any church ever faces: change. One of the rumors circulating was that I only accepted the invitation of the search committee if they could guarantee that Roger would be brought as the music minister; this is not true. But I certainly felt he should be considered along with other candidates. The committee decided he was the pick of the crop and he eventually came as Minister of Music.

For many years, Sunday School had been the driving force behind church growth. It was now evident that position had been taken over by Sunday morning worship, which was usually the decisive factor in how people decided to join a church. The Sunday morning worship became one of the primary drawing cards for Broadway and we did begin to grow. "Growing pains" has come to be an accepted term that has usually been accepted as indicating: you can't have the one without the other. It's just a part of life; it's just a part of church.

SOME INCIDENTS AND INSIGHTS

Deacons' meetings were usually lively and productive. About six months into my ministry, I was asked in one of those meetings to give the basic impression I had of the congregation. I thought for a moment and then said something like, "Well, one certainly has to be impressed with the high quality of leadership to be found in this congregation. I believe it is far above the average. I think I agree with the person who told me, 'We have lots of chiefs and very few Indians.'" From the back of the room, someone interrupted with: "Would you mind pointing out the Indians?" The laughter that filled the room was the only response I thought was necessary.

One of the members wanted to do something in memory of her husband and, through a long process of deliberation and investigation, she decided she wanted to give a large stained-glass window for the front of the sanctuary. Until that time, the front had been dominated by three large heavy draperies, the center one of which opened to disclose the baptistry. The look was almost identical to that of the seminary's chapel. When rumors began spreading that such a change was being considered, the opposition was significant. One of the members, an artist, arrived at a method of presentation for the idea. At a called business meeting one night a few months later, people assembled in the sanctuary to find that very large white paper coverings had replaced the draperies. An information folder gave a picture of the proposed window and explained each item in the large center section and the two smaller narrow sections on each side. When the presentation ended, the lights went out and from a projector in the balcony each of the sections was filled with images of the proposed windows. It was stunning and literally transformed the feel of the sanctuary. The new stained-glass windows were installed a few months later.

What I always loved about Broadway was that most meetings were lively events with open and free discussion and, usually, a generous helping of laughter. One of the members of the church was Elizabeth Fuller, the widow of the former president of Southern Seminary. Everyone fell in love with her and Pat and I were no exceptions. She was very much alive in her later years and I remember her telling the story of how proud she was that when the Charleston came out, she was among some of the first to learn the dance! (Now, in that day, you did not hear that from many Baptists!) In one business meeting, some item was under discussion (I have forgotten the specifics) and one of the members said, "I think we ought to approve this measure because our Pastor has recommended it and we should follow his leadership." Mrs. Fuller got the floor: "Well, I think that all depends on where he is going to lead us!" Much laughter followed and I always like to add, "She almost got a standing ovation." Whatever it was, the measure passed.

For several years I taught a young adult Sunday School class. I don't know when I have ever enjoyed any teaching experience so much. We had an average attendance of about fifty; discussions were lively and honest at times to the point of hilarity! I think it was an illustration of the ideal setting for real learning and getting to know one another. Of course, you will always be able to find someone who can add a negative note to almost any situation. A person who taught one of the children's classes in Sunday School came to see me complaining that several of the parents attending my class were always late in dropping off their children for her class. "Please inform them they need to get their children to Sunday School on time." I never had been a "Now hear this!" minister but I responded to her request (demand?) as best I could. "I appreciate the fact that these busy parents get themselves and their children ready for Sunday School and come – even if they are a few minutes late. I can't think of a thing I could say that would be helpful." (I did know that she and her husband ran a tight ship with their son; she was convinced that everyone else could do the same.) She left still not convinced that appreciation and encouragement ought to rule the day.

While I was at Broadway, it seemed we were always in a building program. Friendship Hall, along with additional classroom space, a new library, kitchen, and parlor, was completed in 1983. New music and office suites and a Family Life Center were occupied in 1992. Someone was willing to fund a much-needed music suite and it certainly was time for some new offices for the staff. We also needed a fellowship hall for dinners and meetings (when I arrived, we were meeting in the basement of the chapel for such meetings). One of these projects called for the relocation of the library in a place of maximum traffic flow. The planners felt they had worked that out but the person in charge of the library was not happy. The library had been in its present location for a long time and it did not need to move. In a Wednesday business meeting she made her case by reading a revised story she called "The Little Library on the Prairie." I had to understand that tradition and place are both very important and much more so as we get older. Change often seems to rule the day to such an extent that it often seems like "everything nailed down is coming loose." I don't think the librarian ever got over her loss of space but the much-improved new library came into being. During the process, I heard that her husband was using the church printing equipment to send a monthly newsletter to all their family members and close friends about the mistakes the pastor and present leadership were making in the life of the church. I continued to be their pastor and tried to make a place for disappointment on the part of members – which is always present in a time of transition.

The phase of the building program involving a family life center apparently brought upsetting news to a few of the church's neighbors and resulted in a lawsuit being filed to stop the project. Of course, that meant we got newspaper coverage about the church building a facility that was going to be disruptive to the tranquility of the neighborhood. One of the most helpful things I ever received in ministry was an hour session from one of the members whose specialty was providing good public relations techniques for businesses and organizations that were dealing with negative publicity. I learned how not to be quoted in the media. Whenever a reporter called, I was instructed to say, "I'm busy at the moment but let me finish up some things and give me a call back in an hour." During that hour I was carefully to frame any responses I wanted to make that related to the neighbors around the church. All reporters were looking for was a word or a phrase that would make a nice headline for his article. For example: "Angry minister doesn't know how neighbors could be so ugly!" It was something I would never say but all the reporter needs is one spoken word. So, I worked carefully to give a generic and low-key response to any question. I never provided any quotable quotes; I was never mentioned in any newspaper article about the conflict between church and community. Compromises were made, the facility was built, and no disruption was ever sited; no further complaints were ever heard. The wild parties in the family life center never happened.

THE SBC CRISIS COMES HOME TO THE SEMINARY AND TO BROADWAY

Southeastern Seminary's trustees were about to appoint a new president and it promised to be one of the fundamentalists in the takeover group. I received a call from one of my Southeastern classmates asking if I would be willing to serve as alumni president for the coming year. It was thought that someone with Southern roots in the present might be of some help in the selection process. I agreed and found myself one week before the trustee's meeting in Wake Forest ready to host the annual alumni meeting. We had been asked to draw up a list of characteristics we would like to see in a new president. We got to work even though the rumor mill let us know that the trustees had already made their selection. The next day, the chairman of the trustees asked me to meet with him. During the conversation, I told him what we had heard and mentioned by name the rumored selection. He then asked, "If _____ were to be selected, do you see anything that would be contrary to anything on the list your committee is drawing up?" I said I didn't think so and his response was: "That is an answer to prayer!" This confirmed that the selection had already been made and our efforts were simply for good public relations.

When I returned to Louisville, it was with a warning that Southern Seminary was next on the hit list. The unanimous response was: "Nothing like that could ever happen here!" But it could. And it did. And Roy Honeycutt, one of the best presidents and persons I have ever known, was out. The process was ugly with the usual name calling, accusations of unbiblical teaching, and whatever it took to accomplish the takeover. I recommend a recent read, *The Kingdom, the Power, and the Glory: American Evangelicals in an Age of Extremism* by Tim Alberta, because it provides a larger context for what occurred in the SBC. In the book, a Guidepost report provides some shocking details about later events in the lives of two of the architects of the fundamentalist takeover. Paige Patterson was fired by Southwestern Seminary in 2018 "for his repeated mishandling of rape cases, including one instance of an outright cover-up." Texas judge Paul Pressler had "mounting legal troubles related to his alleged sexual assaults of underage males."[11]

The theme of the 2022 Southern Baptist Convention, displayed on literature and banners, was "JESUS: the Center of it All." (Often during the conflict, you might have thought it was a book.) My contention, which sounds like heresy, is that we are not people of the book but people of the Person. The earliest confession of faith was "Jesus is Lord" and Jesus' only invitation was "Follow me." His last command to his disciples (Matthew 28:19-20) was to "make disciples" which means "make learners." It is obvious in Matthew that Jesus is the Teacher to whom the learners are to listen. When you carefully read Matthew's Gospel you discover that he presents Jesus as the new Moses; in Matthew chapters five through seven we have "The Sermon on the Mount" which has

---

11 Tim Alberta, *The Kingdom, the Power, and the Glory* (New York: Harper, 2023), 365.

obvious parallels to Moses receiving the Ten Commandments on Mount Sinai. Recently, I read an article by a seminary president who boasted that his school produced students who could go out "preaching the Bible." I would have thought the goal would be to send out students who could go out preaching the Good News: Jesus the Anointed One, the Messiah. (The unpacking of that would require another book.)

Our church was soon blacklisted by the seminary; no one who worked in any capacity at the seminary could belong to a church that ordained women to ministry. We lost a prominent member and his family as a result and the door was off-limits for even student visitation to our services. The process was in the works, and shortly after I retired, the church withdrew from the Southern Baptist Convention and joined the Cooperative Baptist Fellowship. They wanted that question settled before the arrival of a new pastor.

UNREST AND A MAJOR DECISION

One of the seminary professors who was a member of Broadway taught classes dealing with conflict in churches. He told me once that almost every pastor experienced a major crisis in the church during his seventh year. Mine came a great deal later. I can't pinpoint the exact date when rumors began to surface about unhappiness with my ministry and the need for a younger minister who could draw young families into the church. Some reported that meetings of the disgruntled were being held in various homes. About that same time, I had put into works the possibility for an outside resource person to lead the church in a self-study and the mapping of future goals and how we might attain them. The plan was rejected primarily due to its cost and, instead, a self-study was to be done by the deacons. Various committees were appointed; the one dealing with church staff drew the greatest amount of interest and some quickly volunteered to be on the committee. I had the feeling this might not be so good. It wasn't.

A kind and gracious member of the congregation offered to pay for me to have some sessions with Wayne Oates, the chair of the Pastoral Care Department at the seminary, and one of my heroes. Dr. Oates had written over fifty books and I had many of them on my shelf including my favorite: *The Struggle to be Free: My Story and Your Story.* My sessions with Wayne can only be described as life- saving. Just being in his presence brought a sense of calm and reassurance. He offered no simple solutions or Pollyanna outcomes. One of his many questions was; might it be time for me to close out my time at Broadway? At that point, it was about eighteen months until I would be sixty-five and eligible for social security. Also, I could not imagine any church that would be anxious to hire a sixty-four- year-old minister. Our fifty-minute sessions were enlightening, provocative, and healing. I left those sessions determined, in my remaining time, not to allow any negativity to enter my sermons or my ministry. He made me realize that most people in the congregation were unaware of this conflict. I began talking with trusted deacons and friends and arrived at a retirement date of January 31, 2001. I would announce my retirement six months in advance. My sessions with Wayne Oates convinced me it was time to get off the train and wander around the station until I found another train for departure into the next place for ministry and service.

A GRAND EXIT THAT REMINDED ME OF AN HILARIOUS BEGINNING

My first Sunday at Broadway was exhilarating for many reasons. The pews were packed and there were many "special" visitors. One of the very special ones was Prof Inman Johnson who had been my speech professor my first year at the seminary and had taught me more about how to use my voice than I ever thought I needed to know: but I did! He was much beloved by his students and I was certainly one of that number. At the conclusion of the service, I did something that I never do. I called on Prof to come forward and give us the benediction. Anyone could have warned me that Prof. didn't give the usual benediction; he never gave the usual anything. I was standing at the front before the microphone; Prof made his way to the front and when he arrived, he faced the congregation, put an arm around my shoulders, and announced, "This is one of my boys." Then he looked at me and said, "The last pastor stayed here thirty years…and if you don't do some fool thing, you might be able to stay here thirty years!" Laughter filled the sanctuary. I couldn't think of a better way to conclude my first service with the congregation: peals of laughter. Prof's benediction followed. My ministry had begun.

For the departure, a banquet had been arranged at a large meeting hall associated with the University of Louisville. A limousine arrived at our front door to transport us to the dinner. It was structured to be a celebration of my ministry and the expression of gratitude of the congregation for my twenty years. It was a moving evening of laughter, tears, and surprises. Our older son Mark did a number from the musical *Charlie Brown* and my younger son, Michael, read a piece he had written titled "Things you don't know about my dad." There were several creative presentations and some very kind words from the chair of the committee that had called me to Broadway. In my brief appreciation comments at the end of the program, I concluded with: "If I had known my departure was going to be this much fun, I would have retired sooner!"

Shortly thereafter, a group of friends invited us to dinner, and presented us with the gift of a two-week Mediterranean cruise in the fall. We had never been on a cruise and we could hardly wait to leave on a trip that included Venice and Rome. We were to depart in November; we all remember the tragedy of 9/11. We thought for certain the trip would be canceled but it wasn't. We were assured all would be well and we left for what was literally the trip of a lifetime. Many people chose not to travel that year and when we arrived in Rome it was deserted! Our tours consisted of very small groups and we were treated to leisurely sight-seeing that would have been the envy of most travelers to such major attractions. There were many highlights but I especially remember our guide at Ephesus who gave us a tour that made us feel we were being escorted by the Apostle Paul. I can close my eyes and still see us seated in St. Mark's Square in Venice enjoying lunch with a few other visitors. The crowds were so sparse wherever we went that it seemed most of the time like a private tour. It was the perfect conclusion to what remains, despite the bumpy ending, two-decades of blessing, challenges, achievement, and enrichment at Broadway in Louisville.

Seven Interim Ministry Journeys
2004-2015

Yahweh, will do all things for me.
Yahweh, your faithful love endures forever...
Psalm 138:8, NJB.

A COMPLETELY DIFFERENT DIRECTION

It didn't take me long to discover that there was not much on the market for a sixty-five-year-old retired Baptist minister. When a friend asked me what my prospects were for some kind of employment, I responded with my favorite faux Latin phrase: *e plurabus goose eggerous*! But I despaired too soon. It was not long until one of my good friends, the pastor at Crescent Hill Baptist Church, recommended me for a position. He served on the board of directors for the Inter-Faith Alliance; they needed an interim director. It was basically a fund-raising position but the opportunity to associate with persons from other faith communities was a major drawing card. The position provided the context for an interesting and demanding year of work. I learned much about the complexities involved in a city the size of Louisville with its challenging problems of drugs and gangs. An afternoon session with the mayor and chief of police revealed a world I didn't even know existed. A new director was found for the Alliance and this brief excursion was over.

Shortly thereafter, a good friend asked if I had ever heard of the Center for Congregational Health in North Carolina. They offered training for serving in an interim position for churches searching for a new pastor. The position was called an "Intentional Interim" and focused on leading the congregation in a self-study before they began the process of looking for a new pastor. The result was that we both traveled to North Carolina for a week's study. The teachers were excellent and the material represented much that I wish I had known in my pastorates. It also introduced me to the Alban Institute with its treasure trove of books on almost everything that goes on in the life of a congregation and concrete suggestions and guidelines for dealing constructively with the conflicts and disruptions that pastors experience. It was the most comprehensive study of congregational life and pastoral leadership I could have imagined. The study continued, mostly from home, for the next two years.

For a better understanding of what was involved in a self-study, below you will find some of the information I gave to a church when it was deciding whether to have an Intentional Interim.

> The Intentional Interim Minister (IIM) enters into a mutually agreeable covenant with the congregation to lead the church and conduct a self-study.

RESPONSIBILITIES:

> To lead through a self-study process to look at five areas of a healthy congregation as they prepare to search for and call the next Pastor. The IIM will help the congregation establish a Transition Team, will train the team, and then facilitate their leading the congregation through the five areas (called Focus Points) of a healthy congregation.
>
> Heritage: reviewing how the congregation has been shaped and formed.
>
> Mission: defining and redefining the sense of purpose and direction.

Leadership: reviewing the congregation's ways of organizing and developing new and effective clergy and lay leadership.

Connections: discovering all the relationships and networks a faith community builds beyond itself.

Future: synthesizing the interim work, activating and training the Pastoral Search Committee, and coaching the committee (as requested) to accomplish its work.

The IIM has an accountability group (usually the Transition Team) designated in the covenant.

There are many more details which are adapted to the specific needs of each congregation. The key ingredients are the weekly meetings (usually on a Wednesday or Sunday night) in which I would make a brief fifteen-minute presentation and then the congregation, gathered at tables of six or eight, would discuss a set of questions and other matters that surfaced. Following the discussion period, a representative selected by each table would make a report to the group. These written reports would be collected and printed for distribution to the entire congregation. The purpose of the interim was to help the church make discoveries about themselves and decide the direction in which they wanted to go. The interim minister never set the agenda or gave the congregation any goals. His was the role of a facilitator.

A NEW PERSPECTIVE ON APPALACHIA

Each church provided a new learning experience for me. My first couple of interims had some rough spots but I think I got much better with some "on site" experience under my belt. First Baptist Corbin was one of my better experiences due in no small part to the fact that Corbin was the home of Kentucky Colonel Sanders first fried chicken restaurant! The church had so many gracious and affirming people and I cannot recall a single major conflict in the process of the interim. I was also discovering the richness and quality of people in Appalachia. My next move was just down the road to First Baptist Church, Williamsburg, where my wife and I lived in the church parsonage. Being on site, except for a brief trip to Louisville every other week, brought a new depth to this interim. We spent almost two years there and our departure was a reluctant one. We made some special friends there including the president of Cumberland College (now Cumberland University) and his wife. The campus is a jewel tucked back off the highway. You would never expect to find such eye popping architecture just down the road from a place called "Dogpatch," the mythological home of hillbilly characters in Al Capp's "Li'l Abner" comic strip. Too many believe this strip gave an accurate description of life and the people in Appalachia. Nothing could be further from the truth. Some of the best and most educated people I have ever known were encountered in these two churches.

MY LONGEST, BUT ALSO ONE OF THE BEST AND TOUGHEST INTERIMS

My next interim took me to Athens, Georgia, for over two years and was filled with new friendships, positive feedback, satisfactory outcomes, and my usual missteps along the way. (Every interim offered new pitfalls and new opportunities for mistakes; I certainly did not want to waste all of them!). Three snapshots of that experience are worth sharing. Following about six months at First Baptist, I gave the deacons my first major written report on what I thought we had accomplished, where I thought we were and what I envisioned for our future work together. After the group of about thirty had time to read the report, I asked: "Does anyone have a question?" "Yes," came a voice from down one of the tables. "Do you think the U of K fans were fair to Tubby Smith?" After the laughter subsided, I replied: "I never get into the two most dangerous subjects for a minister: sports and politics. But, strictly off the record, if you promise to keep it a secret, I will tell you: I don't think the fans have been fair to any coach – if he does not produce a winning team with a winning season."

Some situations were not so humorous and it was my duty to bring a little lightness to the situation. Almost a year after my arrival, a member dropped by the office one day with a question. He was a regular Sunday attender and I could tell that he did have a concern. "Pastor," he began, "you preach so much about grace. I want to know when you are going to start preaching about sin." I paused, giving myself time for a reflective response, and asked, "What sins did you have in mind?" That led to a very good discussion about my philosophy of sermons and the nature of the Gospel. I had never found preaching about sin to be very productive because the sins we all want to hear about are usually someone else's. I believe that in an atmosphere of grace, mercy, and forgiveness we are more likely to recognize where we have missed the mark and fallen short of the glory God intends for our lives. The pounding of the pulpit and the waving of the Bible (in the days gone by) usually only put people who needed to reflect on the defensive. We parted on good terms and a mutual understanding of what we both agreed was the best way to reach people with the "good news" of the Gospel.

Not every situation was so pleasant and one was very disruptive for a small group of the members. When I came to the church, there was an early morning service at eight-thirty on Sunday morning. The former pastor had begun this service without the approval of the deacons because he said he was interested in reaching the students at the University of Georgia. (The campus was located a little over a stone's throw from the church.) My first question was: Who thought students were going to get up that early on a Sunday morning? The major problem involved those who had the responsibility for planning and leading the service. Neither the pastor or the Minister of Music were ever consulted, nor were they invited to the closed prayer meeting prior to the service. The pastor was expected to deliver a sermon and a closing prayer. As I began to explore the reason for the present situation,

I discovered that the person who led the music had no musical training. He could not read music and simply played his guitar from the heart. And, I can tell you, his heart had a very loud beat! The music program at the church was first class and the early service did not reflect very much about the church. (The music was more in the style of the later praise bands.) What was most disturbing was that when the music leader and his wife were asked to be greeters on Sunday mornings following the early service, they explained that they could welcome people to the early service but could not welcome them to the eleven o'clock service. It was not "their kind" of service.

In one of my weekly meetings with the Transition Team, I discussed this situation with the team and, unwisely, expressed my displeasure with the early service. My first complaint was that I saw no need for it and, as usually happens, we really had developed two churches. One member "took me on" and I use that term advisedly. He was known for being very confrontational; one person referred to him as a trouble maker. My experience has shown that it is not productive to have an "out of sorts" member on the team; making the decisions for the interim process is difficult enough without this built-in stumbling block. Regretfully, we had several heated sessions. I did my best to calm the waters and to do what I could to continue with the early service. The details are not important but the results are: Shortly after the conclusion of my interim, the deacons voted to discontinue the early service and my unhappy team member left the church. I'm convinced this only made things easier for the new pastor.

My big regret is that, in this interim, I violated one of my basic rules. After the new pastor came, I returned to do a study on one of my books. The rule is: cut all ties with the church; give the new pastor time and space to establish himself; give no advice or recommendations of any kind. It is so easy to make this kind of mistake, especially in a church that has captured your heart.

NEW CHALLENGES ARE SIMPLY A PART OF THE PROCESS

One interim (name withheld) offered a new, but not unexpected, challenge. Not everyone is in favor of doing an intentional interim; it does require an impressive majority before it should be attempted. In one church, I thought all was going well until I discovered that one of the Sunday School classes had vetoed the situation and none of them had attended any of the Wednesday night discussion sessions. I was asked to visit with the class on a Sunday morning. I did and learned a few more things. The teacher of the class did not like the deacon structure of the church and thought there ought to be elders who had more power and control in setting plans and priorities. This was a listening session for me. It was especially difficult because the father of the teacher of that class was one of the most outspoken supporters of the interim process. The study continued with no major disruption from the class of dissenters.

One other thing marred my interim there. I was to be in the office for most of the week. I hardly ever got a phone call and any visits from members was set up from conversations on Sunday and Wednesday. Sitting in the office all day on Friday got to be a great drag. In my eighteen months with the church, I never got a single phone call on Friday. I told the business manager, who really oversaw the running the church, that I would be happy to be "on call" each Friday but it simply was too much to sit there all day. This followed a flair up I had with my blood pressure. My doctor thought my schedule was just too full for a person approaching eighty. I brought his recommendations into the meeting with the business manager. He didn't approve of my plan but agreed. Our relationship was never the same after that.

DEEP IN THE HEART OF TEXAS

When I told one of my friends, who was from Texas, that I was going to Austin for an interim, he began a litany of praise for the only state that was once a country! He loved Texas and had several family members who lived there. After I had completed my almost two-year stint in "the promised land" I returned to give my friend a report. It was short and to the point: "Everything you said about Texas being a great place is true! We had a great time in a great place with some truly great people." He just beamed and couldn't resist adding: "Remember. I told you so."

A former member of the congregation had made available a small apartment on his property for the interim pastor. It was on one of the tall hills that surround Austin and provides a panoramic view of the city. It was a relatively short distance from the church and we soon learned "the back way" that kept us off "Mopac." It was called the "Mopac Expressway" but we found nothing about it to be express. With 50,000 university students and the usual travel that comes with a capital, I liked to call it the "Mopac Creepway." However, we learned to navigate and when to use the expressway when it could be just that. One thing we learned was that when we asked how far a certain place was, the reply would usually be "just down the road." That could mean anywhere up to 200 miles away! Texas is a big place!

In one of our Wednesday night sessions, Pat was seated at a table with several others, as I enjoyed some of the lighter moments in my presentation. At the conclusion of one of my stories, a woman turned to Pat and asked, "Is he always this silly?" "No," Pat responded, "sometimes he's worse." I had always believed that almost every serious subject needed a little bit of comic relief. I recently rewatched Spielberg's *Lincoln*. In one scene, during the Civil War, he interrupted a cabinet meeting to tell one of his humorous stories. Some shook their heads in disbelief, but most appreciated what Lincoln once replied in response to criticism of his stories: "If I did not have a little bit of laughter in these terrible times I would die."

Highland Park turned out to be a happy and productive experience. Perhaps my years of experience had further mellowed me but everything seemed to go smoother and there were fewer big bumps in the road. We departed, grateful and most appreciative for our time in the place where "the stars at night are big and bright." In our experience, just about everything was big and bright and we still have some friendships that go back to those days.

AN INTERIM INTERRUPTED BY THE WORST EXPERIENCE OF MY LIFE

First Baptist Morehead was one of the easier interims. There were no major problems, it was basically a healthy church, and they simply wanted to pause, take a look at themselves, take time to talk with each other about their past and future, and determine the best way forward for this church located in the same city as Morehead State University. The only negative: it is quite a distance from Louisville and I made the trip twice a week for well over a year. The Transition Team met on Sunday following worship and I returned early on Wednesday for meetings in the afternoon and the self-study groups following the Wednesday night suppers.

For this relatively small church, the music program was excellent. The choir director was a part of the music department at the university and some of the students sang in the choir. The highlight of the music on Sunday was frequently the pianist who was one of the most talented I have ever heard. His improvisations of standard hymns were incredible. Sometimes, he would do a classical jazz version of one of the old standards and you would have to listen carefully to recognize the source. It was one of those churches where the prelude, the offertory, and the postlude kept the congregation in their seats, literally all ears.

On Wednesday April 24, 2013, I was on the Lexington bypass making my way back to Louisville after spending the day in Morehead. My cell phone rang and I answered to these words from Michael, my younger son: "Dad, find a place to pull over and stop. I need to tell you something." I explained that there was no place to pull over until I got off the by-pass. "What do you need to tell me?" After a pause and more hesitation, he finally told me: "When Mark's housemate returned after his day's work, he discovered that Mark had taken his life." We knew that Mark was bi-polar and on medication. What we did not know was that the medication made him "feel so awful" (his words) that he had stopped taking it. Everything I have read since, confirms that once this happens, the risk of suicide escalates dramatically. I felt nothing as I covered the remaining miles to Louisville. It was the worst experience of my life.

First Baptist Morehead was gracious and supportive. I agreed to return as interim in five weeks. The prayers, support, and financial help we received from Broadway were far beyond what anyone would ever expect. Pat and I could not have survived without this caring community putting its loving arms around us. (Later, out of this experience came one of my books, *Surviving a Son's Suicide*. I felt I had to put something in print. I had to tell the story.) So much of this time is a blur but what stands out clearly is the fact that so many people simply stood beside us through it all. That made the difference.

Mark died, heavily in debt, and with no insurance. He owed his housemate almost $3,000 he had borrowed in recent months. The cost of bringing the body to Louisville from Atlanta, the purchase of a grave at Cave Hill, and the erection of a tombstone were significant. We never told anyone the circumstances but financial help poured in from all directions and with what we were able to contribute plus all the gifts, we fully covered all expenses. We had never had such an outpouring of this kind of help in all of its dimensions; deep appreciation and gratitude carried us through the experience.

When I returned to Morehead, it was therapeutic for me to be able to speak from the pulpit with honesty and grief in a sermon I titled "When All the Lights Go Out." The congregation listened to the sermon with compassionate hearts and I experienced the same kind of love and support I had received from Broadway. This for me has always been church at its highest and best. I don't believe any other organization is able to provide the kind of support that a faith-based community is able to offer. I completed my work with the congregation, a new pastor was called, and I have always included Morehead on my list of special blessings.

A MOST UNEXPECTED INTERIM

Following a brief interim (not mentioned in the above), that did not go so well, I concluded it was time to hang up that hat and devote myself to my writing and just being a "regular" member at Broadway. I wasn't very far into my unannounced retirement when our pastor announced his decision to accept a college teaching position. The pastor spoke of experiencing "burn out" in ministry; he cited several friends his age who were experiencing the same thing. He was not forsaking his calling; his calling simply took him in another direction.

The decision Broadway had to make was whether to immediately begin searching for a new pastor or to have an intentional interim to provide the opportunity for reflection, conversation, and planning together for the future. They soon discovered that this was not an inexpensive venture. They looked in the bargain basement and decided that I had the training and the experience to provide them with a first-quality low-cost experience. The chair of deacons was a person with the necessary skills and wisdom to lead the church through this wilderness period. I knew it would be a privilege to work with her in a new role that would not bear the label of former pastor.

It took a while to get things sorted out and to overcome some reluctance on the part of some members of the congregation.

At the conclusion of our study, the associate pastor told me that someone said to her after the announcement of my being chosen for this position: "The last thing we need is an eighty-year-old interim minister." At the conclusion of my tenure, she said he came to her with the comment, "I was wrong." I understood exactly his initial reaction. Sometimes, however, it takes some years to accumulate the life experiences, coupled with the training, to prepare for this unusual and demanding consulting role.

In my interims, I usually preached every Sunday morning. The text and themes of the sermon provide the context for the studies I am doing with the congregation. Since there were women ministers on the staff who had been preaching, I finally negotiated preaching three times a month with these ministers alternating months. Setting the tone and mood for the studies is an important strategy. The congregation would be confronting issues and having discussions on subjects that had never crossed their paths. In taking a survey to determine the time for our teaching/discussion sessions, the best time for most people was Sunday following the morning service. This was the time selected; it was preceded by a luncheon. We always concluded by 2:00 p.m. We had a consistently large attendance; the sessions were highly productive.

However, (and there are always a few "howevers" in every interim process), there was a staff problem that needed to be resolved before the arrival of a new pastor. I cannot reveal any confidential information, but only need to say that the individual involved was not entirely happy with her present role. She really had dreams of being a pastor. The staff had complained that she was not pulling her weight as a staff member and some of the congregation was unhappy with her job performance. A personal conflict developed due to one of her job descriptions as the "Minister of Church Information." When I gave my mid-point report on the self-study and the plans for its completion, it was shaped into an attractive and eye-catching six-page document by a secretary. She was chastised by the minister of information for not first submitting my report to her for approval. The secretary told me about the rebuke and I met with the minister to let her know that it was my report and in all my interims, no one had ever audited or edited what I presented.

This was a very difficult situation but we knew we could not leave this problem situation for the new pastor. In the continuing conversations the deacon chair and I had with the minister, it was obvious that she could not continue in this position. Staff meetings had brought to light other what I term "failures to function" and her unhappiness with her present role was obvious. Negotiations began for a departure that would be orderly and fair. She was offered severance pay of three months full salary and our promise of recommendations for future positions. The goal of our negotiations was to handle everything in a redemptive spirit that would keep the best future open for all concerned. The end of the story is that this staff member found an excellent pastoral position and reports came back that she was doing an excellent job. Some members of Broadway were quite upset at her being "forced out." Two of her close friends left the church. However (that word again), the consensus was that what was done resulted in the best thing for everyone concerned.

The self-study concluded, final reports were made, and the Search Committee was hard at work. The chair of the committee told me, "There are not many options out there for the kind of pastor we're looking for." My response to him was, "You don't need a lot of options. You just need the right person." He said, "Well, I can tell you the best of the lot," and he gave me the name. Further interviews were held with that candidate, resulting in the minister and his wife being brought to Louisville for a weekend. In one of the meetings with staff prior to the Sunday service in which the "trial sermon" was preached, my conclusion was simply: "I think he is the perfect match for Broadway." Others came to the same conclusion and he has just completed over five years of productive ministry.

This final note will sound out of place to some but at the conclusion of my last interim and my retirement at the age of eighty-three, it was a much- needed affirmation in the light of the less than perfect ending to my twenty years at Broadway. At the conclusion of the final service before the arrival of the new pastor the following week, the deacon chair thanked me on behalf of the congregation and presented Pat and me with the gift of a week in Colonial Williamsburg. As I accepted the envelope and thanked her, the congregation rose for a standing ovation. No one except another pastor can begin to understand how much this meant. Instead of feeling as though THE END had been announced, it felt like affirmation and encouragement to continue my journey. And that is exactly what I did.

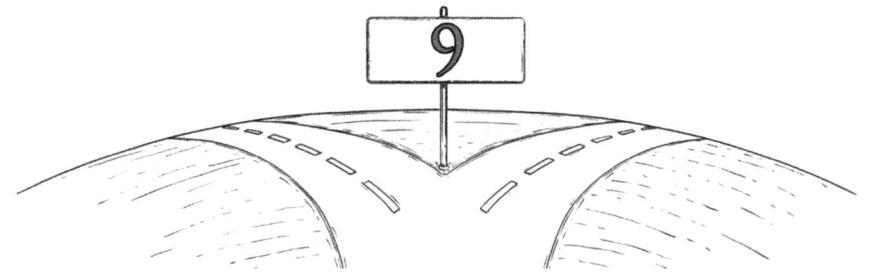

Books and Discoveries
2015-2025

*Send out your light and your truth;
they shall be my guide.* Psalm 43:3, NJB.

A WHATEVER READING PROGRAM

Preaching about forty-five times a year and leading about the same number of Bible studies necessitated a reading program heavy in theology and pastoral care. It always included a "whatever" program that sent me off in all directions and, to this day, always provides me with a book that I love reading. If someone were to peruse my library shelves they might conclude: "this man is a heretic!" My pet peeve is people who will read a book until they come to something with which they disagree and then they will discard the book. There are very few books on my shelf that bring a one-hundred-percent agreement from me. But from those same books, I have found much enlightenment and enrichment. If I only read books that echo everything I already hold fast and I only listen to people who confirm everything I already believe, I have constructed a wall around the possibility for any new perspectives or corrections in faulty thinking. I am like Chester A. Riley in the old "Life of Riley" radio show who repeatedly said, "My head is made up!" The biggest problem with this attitude is that there is no room for conversation, dialogue, or exchange of different points of view. Sounds like the lack of dialogue in modern politics, doesn't it? It only produces deadlock, division, and conflict.

Two reads from the past illustrate my whatever approach. I read David Bentley Hart's *Atheist Delusions*.[12] It is thoughtful, historically accurate, intelligently written, and easily understandable. (His translation of the New Testament is my current choice for daily Bible readings.) I also read along with his book, *The Four Horsemen* by Christopher Hitches, Richard Dawkins, Sam Harris, and Daniel Dennet[13] who are leading the charge in what is called "The New Atheism." It is not surprising that some of the criticisms they level at the church are the same criticisms I have! There is much in their book which calls for thoughtful responses (which I believe Hart delivers). Many of their complaints about the church are taken from the worst examples. They do not waste much time with Christianity at its best (if they believe there is such a thing). I also read *God and the New Atheism:* A Critical Response to Dawkins, Harris, and Hitchens.[14] This kind of reading is meant to lead one to critical thinking which is always the basis for any kind of dialogue. Democracy cannot survive without a public willing to do some critical thinking and engage in rational dialogue.

I credit one of my very best friends ever, Perry Bramlett, with opening the doors to a wider world of books as we perused used bookstores; one in Cincinnati with several floors of books was his favorite. These excursions turned out to be one of the joys of my life and the source for workshops that continue to provide some of the most enjoyable times in my "retirement."

---

12 David Bentley Hart, *Atheist Delusions* (New Haven: Yale University Press, 2009).
13 Christopher Hitches, Richard Dawkins, Sam Harris, and Daniel Dennet, *The Four Horsemen* (New York: Random House, 2019).
14 John F Haught, *God and the New Atheism* (Louisville: Westminster John Knox, 2008).

A FEW NONFICTION RECOMMENDATIONS

I give you a few of some of my most profitable, enjoyable, and enriching reads in historical writings.

Andrew Roberts, *Churchill: Walking with Destiny.* A delightful tome running over nine hundred pages of text that reads like a novel. There never was a character who, as a newspaper reporter, could in the middle of a Boar War battle, with the bullets flying, walk around shouting: "Keep cool, men. This will be interesting for my paper."[15] There never was a greater speech maker, writer, or leader in time of war.

Paul Johnson, *Churchill.* A shorter (165 pages), but superb biography that brings Churchill to life with dozens of quotes and speeches including this gem: "As a young politician, he found himself sitting at dinner next to Violet Asquith, daughter of the then chancellor of the exchequer. Responding to her question, he announced: 'We are all worms. But I really think I am a glow worm.'"[16]

Eric Larson, *the Demon of Unrest: A Saga of Hubris, Heartbreak, and Heroism at the Dawn of the Civil War.*[17] A page turner about Fort Sumter, Abraham Lincoln and the many people who take part in this high drama.

Karl Weber, ed., *Lincoln: A President for the Ages.*[18] Based on the Steven Spielberg Film. A series of essays that explores the past with questions about how Lincoln would have responded to some modern-day issues.

---

15 Andrew Roberts, *Churchill: Walking With Destiny* (New York: Penguin Books, 2018), 67.
16 Paul Johnson, *Churchill* (New York: Viking, 2009), 3.
17 Eric Larson, *Demon of Unrest* (New York: Crown, 2024).
18 Karl Weber, ed., *Lincoln: A President for the Ages* (New York: Public Affairs, 2012).

Bob Drury & Tom Clavin, *Valley Forge*.[19] This book enables you to feel what it must have been like to be at Valley Forge in a pivotal moment in American history.

Joseph J. Ellis, *American Dialogue: The Founders and Us*.[20] Enables you to join in a conversation with Jefferson, Adams, Madison, and Washington.

Joseph J. Ellis, *His Excellency George Washington*.[21] A short (275 pages), well-written, enthralling biography of just about everybody's favorite hero.

Sarah Vowell, *Lafayette in the Somewhat United States*. The incredible story of the nineteen-year-old wealthy Frenchman who volunteered his services, was commissioned a major general, and became one of the heroes of the Revolutionary War and the son Washington never had. When he returned to the United States at the invitation of President Madison on the golden anniversary of American independence, eighty thousand fans turned out in New York to welcome him.[22]

Joseph J. Ellis, *First Family: Abigail and John Adams*.[23] Nowhere else in history is there anything like the material Ellis had to work with when he wrote this book: he read all the roughly twelve hundred letters they wrote to one another! It's as exciting as any novel you will ever read with many historical milestones, including the part Abigail Adams played in the mending of the broken relationship between Adams and Jefferson.

---

19   Bob Drury & Tom Clavin, *Valley Forge* (New York: Simon & Schuster, 2018).
20   Joseph J. Ellis, *American Dialogue: The Founders and Us* (New York: Alfred E. Knopf, 2018).
21   Joseph J. Ellis, *His Excellency George Washington* (New York: Vintage Books, 2005).
22   Sarah Vowell, *Layette in the Somewhat United States* (New York: Riverhead Books, 2015), 3.
23   Joseph J. Ellis, *First Family: Abigail and John Adams* (New York: Vintage Books, 2010).

Bret Baier, *To Rescue the Constitution: George Washington and the Fragile American Experiment.*[24] We are given a seat at the chaotic table when George Washington becomes president of the Constitutional Convention. The book emphasizes the quiet, steady leadership that was needed at a time when many simply wanted to revise the Articles of Confederation and continue as a separate group of independent states.

Ted Widmer, *Lincoln on the Verge: Thirteen Days to Washington.* The election was on November 6 and the inauguration was not until March 4. On February 11 Lincoln was to begin a ten-day train journey from Springfield to Washington. On February 9, the Confederate delegates meeting in Montgomery, Alabama, elected Jefferson Davis president.[25] "A joke going around town (Washington) proposed that the government rearrange the letters of its own name, replacing "United" with "Untied."[26] "Alan Pinkerton later claimed that the day before the journey was to begin, he received 'very decisive information' that Lincoln was to be assassinated in Baltimore.'"[27]

Erik Larson, *The Splendid and the Vile: A Saga of Churchill, Family, and Defiance During the Blitz.*[28] A review from *Forbes* and a line from *Boston*.com printed in the first pages of the book capture all that needs to be said: "A compelling story about Churchill and the war, told with so many keen insights you feel as though you are riding in the limo with him and watching the bombing runs from a first-person vantage point." "Cinematic…makes you feel like you are there."

---

24 Bret Baier, *To Rescue the Constitution: George Washington and the Fragile American Experiment* (New York: Mariner Books, 2023).
25 Ted Widmer, *Lincoln on the Verge: Thirteen Days to Washington* (New York: Simon and Schuster Paperbacks, 2020),104.
26 Ibid, 57.
27 Ibid, 107.
28 Erik Larson, *The Splendid and the Vile: A Saga of Churchill, Family, and Defiance During the Blitz* (New York: Crown, 2022).

Thomas S. Kidd, *Benjamin Franklin: The Religious Life of a Founding Father*. This book could almost be titled, *Things You Never Knew About Benjamin Franklin!* These lines on the back cover summarize the contribution of the book: "Based on rigorous research into Franklin's voluminous correspondence, essays, and almanacs, this fresh assessment of a well-known figure unpacks the contradictions and conundrums that faith presented in Franklin's life."[29]

Ron Chernow, *Alexander Hamilton*. In a section preceding the text called *Praise for Alexander Hamilton*, I added mine: "An eyebrow raising and jaw dropping book." Other comments are: "Alexander Hamilton has been overshadowed by the founding fathers he served under, notably George Washington and Thomas Jefferson. Ron Chernow's magisterial new biography will certainly change that. The first must-read biography of 2004" (John Freeman). "'The life of Alexander Hamilton was so tumultuous that only an audacious novelist could have dreamed it up.' Such is the assessment of Ron Chernow in this splendid new biography of Hamilton" (Steve Raymond).[30]

THE IMPORTANCE OF WORDS AND THEIR ARRANGEMENTS

Whenever a sermon failed to communicate the message of the text, I usually discovered a problem with the arrangement and flow of the sermon. Mystery writers who are word masters provide one of the best arrangements of the words places to find models for both. Anybody can write: "It was a dark and stormy night." But very few have captured a rainstorm like Josephine Tey in *The Man in the Queue*.[31]

29 Thomas Kidd, *Benjamin Franklin: The Religious Life of a Founding Father* (New Haven: Yale University Press, 2017).
30 Ron Chernow, *Alexander Hamilton* (New York: Penguin Books, 2005).
31 Josephine Tey, *The Man in the Queue* (New York: A Touchstone Book, 2007), 86.

A light rain felt across the window-pane with stealthy fingers. The end of the good weather, thought Grant. A silence followed, dark and absolute. It was as if an advance guard, a scout, had spied out the land and gone away to report. There was the long, far-away sigh of the wind that had been asleep for days. Then the first blast of the fighting battalions of the rain struck the window in a wild rattle. The wind tore and raved behind them, hounding them to suicidal deeds of valour. And presently the drip, drip from the roof began a constant gentle monotone beneath the wild symphony, intimate and soothing as the tick of clock. Grant's eyes closed to it, and before the squall had retreated, muttering into the distance, he was asleep.

It's not just what you say, it's how you say it. No one ever expressed this truth any better than Mark Twain in his well-known public domain quote: "The difference between the right word and the almost right word is the difference between lightning and a lightning bug." Writers who say it well have many times come to my assistance (subconsciously) as I have struggled with exactly how I needed to express a particular idea in the sermon. And, of course, Winston Churchill and Abraham Lincoln remain two of my best teachers on the right word, in the right place, at the right time. Good mystery writers provide excellent examples of how to end a sermon. If a mystery simply concludes with "the butler did it," the story ends with a thud. What if it concludes with something like this: "The case had been solved but the inspector felt many of his questions had been left hanging in the air. He found it necessary to continue exploring and re-thinking because there was simply too much more that needed discovering."

I found endings like this (one I fabricated) helpful when dealing with texts like Luke 19:1-10 that discusses Jesus' encounter with Zacchaeus. Jesus inviting himself to lunch in the home of a wealthy tax collector with obvious ties to Rome, was not a minor incident. A conclusion with phrases like: "What the story teaches us in our world today is…" masks the complexity of larger issues that finally result in Jesus' arrest. What about this kind of conclusion:

> I have often wondered what Jesus' disciples talked about as they journeyed back home that day. Their discipleship had involved many surprises and this was one of the biggest. It was a luncheon to remember. I'm convinced they must have had many of the same questions we have. What is our relationship and our obligation to people who are literally up a tree and out on a limb? How far do we need to go with this compassion and outreach thing? I don't know about you, but I'm going to have to continue to think about this.

One of my homiletics professors said that a sermon ought always to leave some work for the people to do. He also said that the highest compliment we could receive after preaching was to have someone say, "I'm going to have to do some thinking about that one." For me, that is better than an "Amen!"

READING IS THE HIDDEN BACKBONE OF SERMON PREPARATION (AND OF KEEPING MY THOUGHTS IN MOTION)

In the Exit Class I taught at Southern, one student proudly announced: "I never read any non-fiction. I only read books that can teach me something." This followed my confession that I always kept a good mystery going as my last read before bed time. My calm response was: "I can think of no better place to learn about the complexities of life and relationships than reading works of fiction by good writers."

My favorite mystery writers all write British mysteries (one of my favorites is Charles Finch, a graduate from Oxford and Yale.) I'm going to give you a short list with a sample quote illustrating some of the wisdom to be found in each. Above all else: they make great, enjoyable, and entertaining reading. (Plus, as you get older, they keep your mind working!)

Charles Todd has written a series of Inspector Ian Rutledge Mysteries set shortly after the First World War. I have learned more about trench warfare and its horrors than from anything else I have ever read. At times, I felt as though I were in those trenches. Also, there is simply a wealth of insights into so many areas of this business of being a compassionate human being:

Rutledge had written many such letters to the families of the dead, and it was a stock phrase, used over and over again by all the officers: *Your son – brother – husband died quickly, without pain, and his final thoughts were of you. He was a brave man, a good soldier, and I was proud to have been his commanding officer...* Even when that man had died screaming in agony, cursing the war and the Germans. A kind lie, a last service for the dead. And those at home had believed the kind lie, because they needed to.[32]

Another favorite series is by Charles Finch and is set in London in the eighteen-fifties. Historical references abound. I learned that Robert Peel introduced the first police force in London in 1829. They were called "peelers" but later the name "bobbies" became their more frequent title. Also, references like this make for an especially informative read:

> Mr. Bernard Rider stopped at each house, collecting the kitchen leavings, flirting along the way. When his cart was full, he sold the leavings – what people called the "wash" – to a mill outside of London, which turned them into food for pigs. Such was the origin of the word "hogwash."[33]

If, on occasion, I'm ready for a wild ride, I pick up a C. J. Box novel featuring Joe Pickett as a game warden in Wyoming. The book has environmental themes and overlapping plot lines that make it the proverbial page-turner. It has some keen insights tucked into its fast-moving story.

---

32 Charles Todd, *No Shred of Evidence* (New York: William Morrow, 2016), 292.
33 Charles Finch, *An Old Betrayal* (New York: Minotaur Books, 2013), 270.

Joe already knew how he was going to play it because he'd played it the same way before. Once he located the home of Kinnison, he'd walk up to the front door and knock. If someone answering to that name opened the door, Joe would say, "I guess you know why I'm here." The subject's immediate response would dictate how things would go from there on.[34]

Of course, there are many of the classic mystery writers that I explore as well. These are my fun, recreational reads. I will mention only a couple more. M. C. Beaton (1936-2019) was known as the "Queen of Crime" and has left behind two great series. One features Agatha Raisin and is set in the English Cotswold's. The other is a series set in the Scottish Highlands and stars Constable Macbeth. They are both series that give you the same feeling: you always regret turning the last page in each of the books. You're always ready for another one.

Another find is not a series that is new. My find of it is what is new. Jacqueline Winspear has written a series about how Maisie Dobbs moves from a maid in an aristocratic London household when she was thirteen, to the prestigious Girton College in Cambridge, to the battlefields of France as a nurse in WWII, to the establishment of her own detective agency. When I began reading the first in the series, *Maisie Dobbs*, I neglected all my other reading and completed the book in record time. It's not like any regular mystery. It is one of those books that enriches your mind, touches your heart, and warms your soul. The wisdom contained in its pages is almost overwhelming. I marked about thirty references I want to copy and save for inclusion in writing and workshops. The following three quotes all come from *Maisie Dobbs*:

> "Truth walks toward us on the paths of our questions." Maurice's voice once again echoed in her mind. "As soon as you think you have the answer, you have closed the path and may miss vital new information. Wait awhile in the stillness,

---

34 C. J. Box, *Wolf Pack* (New York: G. P. Putnam's Sons, 2019), 55.

and do not rush to conclusions, no matter how uncomfortable the unknowing."[35]

"My, my young lady. You *have* been busy. All I can remember of Latin is the end of that verse: 'First it killed the Romans, and now it's killing me!'"[36]

"But remember, Maisie, remember, truth also came to us as individuals so that we might have a more intimate encounter with the self." Maurice pointed a finger and touched the place where Maisie's heart began to beat quickly. "What is there in your heart that needs to be given light and understanding?"[37]

I always keep a couple of other "I need to read these" books beside my reading chair. They come from anywhere and everywhere. I'm always interested in the remainder section at any bookstore and I also browse Half Price Books. I have a membership at Barnes and Noble that provides free mailing for books I order. The Sunday New York Times Book Review has also provided some great reads. My current two serious reads are: *"Reading the Constitution: Why I Chose Pragmatism, Not Textualism"* by Stephen Breyer.[38] This is not an easy read, but in the context of so much discussion on the national level, I felt I needed some perspective on the two major points of view. My other current read is *Wide Awake: The Forgotten Force that Elected Lincoln and Spurred the Civil Way* by Jon Grinspan. I had never heard of this antislavery youth movement "that marched America from the 1860 election to the Civil War" (from the inside front dust cover). Reviewers contend it has much to say to us today. The last line in the Preface certainly got my attention: "The question the Wide Awakes asked

---

35 Jacqueline Winspear, *Maisie Dobbs* (New York: Soho Press, 2019), 32.
36 Ibid, 91.
37 Ibid, 222.
38 Stephen Breyer, *Reading the Constitution: Why I Chose Pragmatism, Not Textualism* (New York: Simon & Schuster, 2024).

in 1860, one with renewed salience today, is what our democracy is capable of."[39]

I am frequently asked if I have gained wisdom with my advancing years and all my reading. My response is always, "Yes, but the kind of wisdom I have gained is the wisdom of realizing how little I know. The more I read (in any field) the greater my ocean of ignorance appears to become. As my knowledge increases so does my awareness of the immensity of all there is to know. I certainly agree with Paul that "I know in part" (I Corinthians 13:12). I'm convinced that the next life will include the adventure of learning, discovery, and exploration of the vast richness of the wisdom of the universe.

THE NUMBER OF BIBLICAL TRANSLATIONS JUST KEEPS GROWING

Dr. Wayne Ward was one of my favorite seminary professors. His preaching was so live-wire that one person quipped: "Dr. Ward doesn't preach; he just clears off a little space and has a fit!" I found him to be one of the most informative and interesting preachers I have ever heard. One Sunday, when he preached at his home church here in Louisville, one of the members commented as she made her exit from the service: "I really get weary of all these new translations of the Bible. I was raised on the King James Version and it is still my favorite. What new translation were you reading from this morning?" Dr. Ward opened the Bible he was holding and let her have a look at his Greek New Testament. If she made a response, I never heard about it.

The business of biblical translation is a complex one to begin with. It is not simply a matter of determining, "This Hebrew/Greek word means this in English." Both the Greek and especially the Hebrew are alive with shades and diversity of meaning. Based on the threescore and ten in Psalm 103:10, some of the rabbis

---

[39] Jon Grinspan, *Wide Awake: The Forgotten Force that elected Lincoln and Spurred the Civil War* (New York: Bloomsbury Publishing, 2024), xviii.

taught that each text of Scripture could be read in seventy different ways, one for each year of our lives. I can testify that Scripture does not speak to me with the same voice and in the same way it did when I was twenty-five. That is the beauty and relevance about the living quality of this timeless collection of writings.

When I was pastor in Waynesboro, Virginia, a member gave me a copy of *The Jerusalem Bible*. I liked it so much that when the *New Jerusalem Bible* was published, I immediately bought it. The KJV translates Romans 8:28: *And we know that all things work together for good to them that love God, to them who are the called according to his purpose.* My reaction to this verse was always: "I don't know that! It just isn't true!" The problem with the translation is that the subject of *good* is *all things*. It is all things that are working for our good. Not in my life! A better, and I believe more accurate translation is from the NJB: *We are well aware that GOD WORKS* (emphasis mine) *with those who love him, those who have been called in accordance with his purpose, and turns everything to their good.*" I also like the more recent translation from *The New Living Translation* (this is NOT the *Living Bible* which is a paraphrase I do not recommend) which reads: *And we know that God causes everything to work together for the good of those who love God and are called according to his purpose for them.*

I know of no modern translation easier to understand for the average reader than *The New Living Translation*. The KJV of Psalm 23 concludes with: *Surely goodness and mercy shall follow me all the days of my life....* The NLT provides the more literal translation: *Surely your goodness and unfailing love will pursue me all the days of my life.* I used that translation in a sermon once with the comment: "God is after you. He is after you with his goodness and unfailing love. Let him overtake you." Matthew 7: 7 in the KJV is *"Ask, seek, and knock."* The NLT puts it in the framework of Jesus' teaching of the need to be persistent in our praying: *"Keep on asking, and you will be given what you ask for. Keep on looking, and you will find. Keep on knocking, and the door will be opened. For everyone who asks, receives. Everyone who seeks, finds. And the door is opened to everyone who knocks."* The context provided by verse 11: *"how much more will your heavenly Father give good gifts to those who ask him",* gives helpful insight to the necessity of "keeping on" in prayer. If we continue asking, we often discover that our asking sometimes changes direction. Our seeking causes us to begin looking in different places. And the doors on which we knock are not the same ones that, in the beginning, we were convinced needed to be opened for us.

The Bible I am currently using for my daily Scripture reading is *The New Testament* by David Bentley Hart. His introduction at the beginning and his postscript to the paperback edition provide some of the most insightful thinking on biblical translation I have ever read. He confesses what every translator needs to confess: "This is not to say that I can pretend to be free of intellectual prejudices: I can only say that I have made every effort not to allow them to interpose themselves between me and the text, even when the result has at some level displeased me."[40] If nothing else, the statement of his principle aim sold me on the book: "My principal aim is to help awaken readers to the mysteries and uncertainties and surprises in the New Testament documents that often lie wholly hidden from view beneath layers of received hermeneutical and theological tradition. And I would hope my translation would succeed, in many places, in making the familiar strange, novel, and perhaps newly compelling."[41]

I found many enlightening and clarifying translations in Hart. What we call "the Lord's Prayer" gives us a couple of new twists: *"Give to us today bread for the day ahead"…*(Matthew 7:11). Day laborers gathered in the market place early in the morning to find employment for the day. They were paid at the end of the day. The family already had to prepare the meal for that supper with the wages received the preceding day. The wages for this day would ensure resources for tomorrow's food. The sec-

---

40 David Bentley Hart, *The New Testament* (New Haven: Yale University Press, 2017), xvi.
41 Ibid, xvi-xvii.

ond example is a little more disturbing: *"And excuse our debts just as we have excused our debtors"* (Matthew 7:12). This means when we ask for forgiveness, we have already forgiven those who need that gift from us. This correlates perfectly with Matthew 7:14: *"For if you forgive men (sic) their offenses, your heavenly Father will also forgive you. But if you should not forgive men (sic), neither will your Father forgive your offenses."* My take on this is that an unforgiving spirit closes the door through which God's forgiveness flows to us.

One of my favorite translation updates comes from Matthew 26:10. It relates to the story of Jesus' anointing at Bethany. A woman comes and pours some very expensive ointment over his head. There is a protest about wasting this ointment instead of selling it and giving the money to the poor. In the KJV, Jesus' response is: *"she hath wrought a good work upon me."* Hart translates it: *"She has done a beautiful deed for me."* (The word translated "good" can also, and in this case should, mean "beautiful"). Matthew 26:13 also gives another example of the value of Hart's translation: KJV: *"Verily I say unto you…"*; Hart's: *"Amen, I tell you, wherever these good tidings are proclaimed, in the whole world, what this woman did will also be told, as a memorial to her."* We would use "amen" at the conclusion of something we wanted to underscore; countless times in the Gospels, Jesus uses "Amen, amen, I say to you…" at the beginning of his comments. It's a "Now hear this!" before the words are spoken. One other note is that throughout the Gospels, Jesus is addressed as Teacher, the most accurate and most frequently used title for Jesus the Anointed (which Hart translates instead of Jesus the Messiah, or Jesus Christ). When Jesus sends Peter and John on ahead to prepare for the observance of Passover, he instructs them to say to a man carrying a vessel of water: *"The Teacher says to you, 'Where is the guest room where I may eat the Passover with my disciples?'"* These are no small matters for a better understanding of Jesus, his teaching, and his ministry. I could give countless more examples of better translations but one will have to suffice. Romans 5:20: *But Law was introduced in order that the transgressions might abound; and, where sin was abundant, grace was superabundant.*

Other translations I recommend for their more literal rendering of the Greek include: Richmond Lattimore's translation of the New Testament is known for its accuracy and fidelity to the original language – and is very readable. The chapter and verses are indicated at the top of each page but not in the body of the text. This helps maintain the unity and flow of each book.[42] *The Restored New Testament* by Willis Barnstone provides a translation of the New Testament with the addition of the Gnostic Gospels Thomas, Mary, and Judas. (A reading of these makes you keenly aware of why they were not included in the New Testament Canon). Robert Alter in an endorsement on a pre-text page, calls Barnstone's translation "almost startling in its freshness…he gives us a set of Gospel narratives that are bold and direct in their simplicity and that show how steeped the first Christians were in the Jewish world from which they derived."

If you are searching for an up-to-date translation of the Hebrew Scriptures (a better term than Old Testament because this implies it is no longer important), nothing is a match for the superb translation by Robert Alter titled *The Hebrew Bible: A Translation with Commentary.*[43] This three-volume set includes the award-winning translation with commentaries to equal or surpass what you can find anywhere else. It can usually be found for less than $100 and makes the perfect gift for a pastor or serious Sunday School teacher. Do not hesitate to buy it for yourself thinking it will be "over your head." It is readable and opens new windows of understanding into the wisdom of the writings we have called "Old" entirely too long. It provides new insights and new appreciation to the Bible used by Jesus and those who first followed him. Why wouldn't we want to

---

42 Richmond Lattimore, *The New Testament* (New York: North Point Press, 1996).

43 Robert Alter, *The Hebrew Bible: A Translation With Commentary* (New York: W. W. Norton & Company, 2019).

read and understand the writings Jesus read and taught in the Synagogue every Sabbath?

The final Bible recommendation I have is one I place on the "you must read this one" list. It is *The Message* by Eugene Peterson.[44] It is a paraphrase subtitled "The Bible in Contemporary Language." It is so true to the text, that I would even recommend it for Bible study; you won't miss the central teachings. However, I always like to keep a solid translation handy for comparison. Peterson's introductions to each book are packed with pastoral wisdom. The freshness and creativity burst forth with the opening verses of Genesis 1:

> *First this: God created the Heavens and the Earth – all you see, all you don't see. Earth was a soup of nothingness, a bottomless nothingness, an inky blackness. God's Spirit brooded like a bird above the watery abyss.*
> *God spoke: "Light!"*
> *And light appeared.*

The Sermon on the Mount comes alive in its practicality, especially in Matthew 7:1 which we usually remember as *Judge not, that you be not judged*. Peterson titles chapter 7 "A Simple Guide for Behavior" and begins it this way:

> *"Don't pick on people, jump on their failures, criticize their faults – unless of course, you want the same treatment. That critical spirit has a way of boomeranging. It's easy to see a smudge on your neighbor's face and be oblivious to the ugly sneer on your own."*

I have used Peterson's treatment of some of the verses in Psalm 36 in a number of sermons:

> *God's love is meteoric,*
>   *His love astronomic,*
> *His purpose titanic,*
>   *His verdicts oceanic,*

---

44 Eugene Peterson, *The Message* (Colorado Springs: Navpress, 2002).

> Yet in his largeness
> Nothing gets lost;
> Not a man, not a mouse,
> Slips through the cracks.

And no one has ever captured the practicality of Paul's famous chapter on love in I Corinthians 13 any better than Peterson. Here are some excerpts:

> *If I speak with human eloquence and angelic ecstasy, but don't love, I'm nothing but the creaking of a rusty gate...So no matter what I say, what I believe, and what I do, I'm bankrupt without love.*

> *Love never gives up.*
> *Love cares more for others than for self.*
> *Love doesn't want what it doesn't have.*
> *Love doesn't strut,*
> *Doesn't have a swelled head,*
> *Doesn't force itself on others,*
> *Isn't always "me first,"*
> *Doesn't fly off the handle,*
> *Doesn't keep score of the sins of others,*
> *Doesn't revel when others grovel,*
> *Takes pleasure in the flowering of truth,*
> *Puts up with anything,*
> *Trusts God always,*
> *Always looks for the best,*
> *Never looks back,*
> *But keeps going to the end.*
> *Love never dies.*

> *...We have three things to do...Trust steadily in God, hope unswervingly, love extravagantly. And the best of the three is love.*

A couple of years ago, someone in one of my workshops gave me a copy of the new biography of Eugene Peterson by Winn Collier: *A Burning in My Bones.*⁴⁵ It is a great read for many reasons, not the least of which is indicated in this brief paragraph from the back cover:

> For Eugene, the gifts of life were inexhaustible: the glint of fading light over the lake; a kiss from his wife, Jan; a good joke; a bowl of butter pecan ice cream. As you enter into his story, you'll find yourself doing the same thing – noticing how the most ordinary things shimmer with new and unexpected beauty.

The biography gives the full story of how he came to write *The Message* and of the overwhelming negative reaction from publishers and retailers. "One response was apocalyptic: 'If we sold this stuff, they'd burn down our bookstore.'"⁴⁶ This kind of response to anything new and fresh is one of the reasons I've always had such a tough time with the ultra-conservative segment of Christianity. NavPress, who'd never published a Bible, finally agreed to do it. "Within months of *The Message* New Testament's release, Eugene became a national figure."⁴⁷

I personally believe that the secret of the translation's success is captured in Peterson's own words: "No one notices or remarks on what I had done in the translation (of *The Message*) – read and listened to the text with my heart, not just with my head – kept the stories in my imagination alive and present all the time."⁴⁸ I went back to my shelves and discovered that through the years I had bought eleven of Peterson's books. One of my favorites remains *Leap Over a Wall: Earthy Spirituality for Everyday Christians.* It is based on the life of David and is another of my must-read recommendations because of paragraphs like this:

> The David story, like most other Bible stories, presents us not with a polished ideal to which we can aspire but with

---

45 Winn Collier, *A Burning in My Bones* (Colorado Springs: Waterbrook, 2021).
46 Ibid, 217.
47 Ibid, 232.
48 Ibid, 246.

a rough-edged actuality in which we see humanity being formed – the *God* presence in the *earth/human* conditions... (David) has little wisdom to pass on to us on how to live successfully. He was an unfortunate parent and an unfaithful husband. From a purely historical point of view, he was a barbaric chieftain with a talent for poetry. But David's importance isn't in his morality or his military prowess but in his experience and witness to God. Every event in his life was a confrontation with God.[49]

---

49 Eugene Paterson, *Leap Over a Wall* (New York: Harper San-Francisco, 1997), 5.

Writing and Workshops

*O Lord my God, you have done many miracles for us.
Your plans for us are too numerous to list.*
Psalm 40:5, NLT.

It was my very good friend Perry Bramlett who set me to writing. It was his encouragement and initial guidance that helped me produce my first three books: a trilogy. "Just begin by taking some of your sermons, revising and editing them for reading instead of hearing, and organize your favorites under a few themes. You'll find a way to make them come together, plus you will also add of number of new insights." So, I got to work, which meant deciding to write for a given period every day. I began that practice and here is what developed. The first three books were published by Parson's Porch Books.[50] The remaining books were published by my current publisher, Energion Publications.[51]

---

50 Ronald Higdon: *From Fear to Faith; But If Not; In the Meantime* (Cleveland, TN: Parson's Porch Books, 2011, 2012, 2017).

51 Ronald Higdon: *Surviving a Son's Suicide; In Changing Times; All I Need to Know I'm Still Learning at 80; Why Doesn't God Do Something? ; Aging is Not Optional; Finding Stability in Uncertain Times; Wonder Where the Wonder Went; Building Bridges in a World of Crumbling Connections; Halo and Hoverboard Not Required; Quitting is Never the Only Option* (Gonzalez, FL: Energion Publishing; 2014, 2017. 2019. 2020, 2021, 2022, 2024, 2024).

From Fear to Faith: The Spiritual Journey from Anxiety to Trust (2011). The book is divided into four sections, with four chapters in each section: Part I: From Fear to Faith in Our Humanity; Part II: From Fear to Faith in Guidance; Part III: From Fear to Faith in God's Ways; Part IV: From Fear to Faith in Eternal Matters.

But If Not: Mastering the Art of Letting Go (2011). Here are the four major divisions of the book and one of the three chapter titles from each: Part I: Reality 101 – Three Little Words That Make for a Disturbing Story: "But if Not" (Daniel 3:13-18); Part II: Responsibility, Not Results – "You Are Among the Called"; Part III: The Bottom Line: Relationships – "A Wrestling Match We All Face" (Genesis 32:22-30); Part IV: Action! Action! Action! – "Right Here! Right Now!" (Matthew 24:45-51).

In the Meantime: Learning to Live in Difficult Times (2012). Again, here are the four major divisions in the book and one of the three chapter titles from each: Part I: What Time Is It? – "You Have to Believe in Endings and Beginnings" (Philippians 3:12-14); Part II: Maintaining Mountaintop Perspectives – "Truth and Love Belong Together" (Ephesians 4:14-16); Part III: In the Meantime Priorities – "Why Did Jesus Eat With Sinners?" (Matthew 9:9-13); Part IV: Discovering Unique Opportunities – "Finding the Growing Edge" (John 16:12-13; Romans 5:1-5).

Surviving a Son's Suicide: Finding Comfort and Hope in Faith, Friends, and Community (2014). In the Preface: "What This Book is All About", I attempt to provide the scope and purpose of the book: "If you are looking for something that makes it possible to avoid the three great words in life and faith – mystery, paradox, and ambiguity – then this book is not for you…This is not a book about triumph or resolution or now it's okay. It's not okay; it never will be okay. Our pain and our questions remain but Pat and I are surviving in the sense that we are attempting to go forward with our lives without Mark's presence." (v). This is a book about what we did and how we are attempting to keep moving forward.

In Changing Times: A Guide for Reflection and Conversation (2014). In his endorsement on the pre-pages to the text, Bill Tuck gives a summary of what this book is about: "(This book) offers a clear and honest appraisal of how to understand the dynamics of congregations and how one can provide helpful leadership during the interim time." I also have tried to write a book that could be helpful during change, conflict, and chaos at any time in any place.

All I Need to Know I'm Still Learning at 80: Things I'm Still Working On! (2017). The title of the book is a reference to Robert Fulghum's classic *All I Really Need to Know I Learned in Kindergarten.* "Fulghum never intended the title to be taken literally but simply attempted to list what he terms some elemental pieces of wisdom that came very early in life." (vii). Some of the chapter titles are: There Are No Trains to Yesterday; The Focus is on Input, Not Outcome; Questions are More Important Than Answers; Truth is a Journey of Discovery; I am Called to be the Best Version of Myself; The First Word is Grace, The Last Word is Grace; There's God to be More.

Why Doesn't God Do Something? A Bold and Honest at the Eternal Question (2017). In a brief book about theodicy (the problem of a world full of evil when there is God who is all powerful and all loving), I attempt to give some basics for reflection and discussion. Many have told me they have found the Conclusion to be one of the most helpful parts of the book: "25 Strategies for Living in a World Where Bad Things Happen."

Aging is Not Optional: How We Handle It is (2019). In the Preface I seek to give the purpose and scope of the book: "In a youth-oriented culture where old age is almost regarded as the unpardonable sin, there is not much space in our daily lives for the discussion of the one reality that is inescapable – aging…My purpose in writing this book is to bring the good news that discussions about aging can bring new purpose, meaning, and hope to all of life – regardless of your present age. This is a book filled with perspectives and suggestions that can make the advancing years truly golden in the sense of satisfaction, meaning, and fulfillment." (vii).

Finding Stability in Uncertain Times: Some Things That Hold Firm When Everything Else Seems to be Falling Apart (2020). "The Sea is So Great, and My Boat Is so Small," the old Breton fisherman's prayer, is an apt description of being overwhelmed by the magnitude of reality and the smallness of the vessel we are doing our best to keep afloat. In the Preface, I provide what I call "Where we will travel in this book" which gives a brief explanation of what each of the twenty-one chapters is about. I provide a concluding quote, the source of which is basically unknown, that brings one important perspective: "We are Easter people living in a Good Friday world."

Wonder Where All the Wonder Went? Clues to Finding Wonder in This World (2021). "When I talk about wonder, I'm talking, among other things, about something that takes you out of yourself, that brings a sense of awe, that lifts you into another dimension of time (or even makes time seem to stand still), that almost brings an electrifying sensation, that brings the assurance of being loved and accepted in a universe full of God's grace." (3).

Building Bridges in a World of Crumbling Connections: The Forgotten Calling that Belongs to All of Us (2022). This is one of my personal favorites and I've not had many calls for workshops using it. I think one of the problems is the assumption that this is about peace- making on an international level. It's not. It is about relationships on all levels within our culture. It's a book that asks the basic question: "Are you reconciled?" and is based on 2 Corinthians 5:18-6:1. A portion of that Scripture reads: *All this is from God who reconciled us to himself through Christ and gave us the ministry of reconciliation; that God was in Christ reconciling the world to himself in Christ…As God's co-workers we urge you not to receive*

God's grace in vain. The book is about how to be a bridge builder in our everyday worlds of multiple relationships. There are many hints and suggestions about "how to" and a large section about the life and amazing writings of a bridge builder who published seven best-selling books of poetry and peace essays before his death at the age of thirteen.

Halo and Hoverboard Not Required: How to Develop a Fully Human Spirituality (2024). I have had many lengthy discussions of why we do not park our humanity at the door when we enter church and we do not make it something apart from our spirituality. A major emphasis in the book is the contention that fully-human spirituality involves the uniqueness that belongs to each of us. It is that embodied uniqueness that is God-given. My conclusion is a quote from Philip Simmons who, at age 35, was diagnosed with ALS. In his book *Learning to Fall: The Blessings of an Imperfect Life,* he challenges us to abandon halo and hoverboard and live a fully human spirituality, a fully human life:

> The imperfect is our paradise. Let us pray, then, that we do not shun the struggle. May we attend with mindfulness, generosity, and compassion to all that is broken in our lives. May we live fully in each flawed and too human moment, and thereby gain the victory.[52]

Quitting Is Never the Only Option: Some Keys to Staying Fully Invested in Living (2024). In the Preface I give the eighteen basic ideas behind each of the chapters that are the keys for making our contribution on whatever level is granted. The publisher on the back cover gives his analysis of the book: "Through the entire discussion, the emphasis is on engaged, invested, fulfilling, inspired living. Not the seeking of perfection, or of reputation, or of superiority to others, but in simply fulfilling your own calling guided by divine inspiration and a thoughtful engagement with the world around you."

---

52   Philip Simmons, *Learning to Fall* (New York: Bantam, 2003), 110.

THE NEW-FOUND JOY OF DOING WORKSHOPS

I have forgotten exactly how the first contact was made, but the Director of Adult Education at Christ United Methodist Church contacted me about the possibility of getting on their list of available persons willing to teach sessions in Adult Sunday School classes. I began with a couple of struggling endeavors and then began to develop a method and procedure that worked for me. These have been on my agenda for several years now and leading two or three sessions on one of my books has been the most gratifying experience of my "retirement" years. The people are gracious and responsive. Being in a smaller room means closer contact with the people; this gives it a slight edge over preaching in a sanctuary. Of course, it is an informal and relaxed atmosphere and the perfect setting for frequent use of humor.

I have done a couple of these at Broadway, but a former pastor needs to be very careful about how he relates to a congregation where a new pastor needs to always be the pastor. Broadway is my "home" church and I am now just a regular member and enjoying the change of being in the pew instead of the pulpit. I'm certain I will continue my workshops at Christ Church as long as I am able and as long as the invitations to do so keep coming.

CONCLUSION

REFLECTIONS AND PERSONAL OBSERVATIONS

Memories appear in flashes of light, in short scenes, in reflections that can make us laugh or bring us to tears. They might come in on a sneaky wave of grief, or be buoyed up from our past by a certain fragrance in the air, or a sound from afar. The essence of memoir, I suppose, is that it could better be described as "re-memory." We don't just look back at an event in our past; we are remembering the memory of what happened. It's a bit like putting the laundry through two wash cycles. (From *This Time Next Year We'll Be Laughing* by Jacqueline Winspear which appears on page 4 in the appendix at the end of Winspear's Maisie Dobbs.)[53]

The most satisfying mysteries I have read are not those that end with conclusions like "the butler did" it, but those that save a few shocking disclosures until last and leave the door open for speculation on what might be coming next. Whenever I was asked about my writing and if I had to be careful that I was not too offensive in anything I wrote, my response was usually, "If you can't raise a few eyebrows, what's the point in writing a book?" I have saved some of my eyebrow raisers for the last so as not to interrupt the flow of the narrative. My reasoning is simple: if I can't be honest now when will I ever be able to do it?

---

53 Jacqueline Winspear, *Maisie Dobbs*.

A SECRET I'VE BEEN KEEPING

My mother kept the secret I mentioned earlier in this book for twenty-five years. I have kept this secret for much longer. When I was in high school, one of my friends told me: "I've just seen your IQ score. You're just average." Without questioning why he had access to this information, I replied, "Well, I guess that means I'll just have to work harder." That's just what I did because being average meant I would always have to put forth more than average effort. My father and mother were always hard workers; the depression had cut short their educations and put them into the workforce when they were young. That hard work ethic continued throughout their lives. We were a poor family in the West End of Louisville. For several years we lived in the LaSalle Apartments, a government housing project at 18th and Algonquin Parkway; later we moved to a "shotgun" house on Ormsby Street (a narrow one-way street). Our house was always spotless. The kitchen linoleum always had that "Glocoat" shine and the kitchenette set sparkled like new. Example: when I came home from college one weekend and sat down in one of the kitchen chairs, I immediately slid right off onto the floor. My mother had waxed the plastic bottom of the chair. My Dad's workshop in the garage was spotless in spite of having a dirt floor. All tools were kept in their assigned place; many were hung on the wooden garage wall with a black outline indicating the exact position for each one. Our very small yard was kept trimmed to perfection and my mother swept the sidewalk in front of the house every morning.

Much in life was beyond my parents' limited agenda, but hard work could be used to provide living and working space that spoke of control, order, and security. It must have been in my genes because I felt that hard work would reap the same benefits for me in spite of the limitations imposed by limited resources. If I could not achieve other things, my academic hard work could bring me a few open doors for college and graduate work. What I kept a secret, except for providing the information on forms for college, seminary, and graduate school admissions, was that I was the Valedictorian of my small high school class and a *Summa cum laude* Georgetown College graduate. I kept it a secret because I didn't want to hear some of the reactions I had gotten on occasion when it had leaked out: "So, does that make you somebody special?" "We always knew you were a geek." I didn't want to be separate from my peers; I just wanted to be "one of the guys."

At the time I entered the ministry, it was the age of "pulpit giants" and the sermon became the major focus of one's pastorate. I believed it was my calling to make certain that when people came to church on Sunday morning, they left with something that gave them courage and hope for living creatively and redemptively in the coming week. It took hard work – and lots of time – to create a twenty-minute biblical, interesting, nourishing, challenging, and listenable sermon. I usually got up no later than five o'clock (sometimes four) and read and studied until it was time to get ready to be in the office at ten o'clock. I never failed to visit all of those in the hospital and nursing homes; I never failed to answer a crisis call for help; I was always able to arrange an office or home visit for those who needed to talk about something. The Tuesday morning staff meeting was high on the agenda as well as other regular meetings that called for my presence. But my highest priority remained that time on Sunday morning when I had the opportunity for interaction with the largest percentage of the congregation I would ever encounter.

I take very seriously Jesus' conversation with Peter found in the concluding chapter of John's gospel. Chapter twenty-one is considered, according to a note in Hart's translation, sort of a "theological coda" and is usually termed the second ending; chapter twenty contains what sounds like final comments following Thomas's great confession of faith. However, chapter twenty-one is a part of the biblical canon and I think Jesus' three questions and his three commands speak to me as a pastor. Three times Jesus asks Peter, "*Do you love me?*" Peter responds with a sounding "Yes" to each question and then is instructed to: (1) "*Shepherd my flocks"; (2) "Feed my flocks"; (3) "Follow me."* (Hart). This is the challenge and the opportunity that presented itself to me every Sunday morning as I looked out into the faces of my congregation and almost heard the question: "What do you have for us today that will nourish and equip us for the week ahead?"

THE PACKAGE IN WHICH WE FIND OURSELVES.

When anyone asks me if I believe in reincarnation, I reply: "I only wish I did. I might have the chance to come back in a bigger package next time." I have always been thin and small of structure. In my youth I tried everything to gain weight: from raw eggs in chocolate milkshakes to using Hadacol. It was a tonic recommend by Roy Rogers so what could go wrong? Well, a lot. It was marketed as a vitamin supplement. It was later discovered it contained twelve percent alcohol which, on the label, was listed as a preservative! With that discovery the market crashed and another vain attempt at weight gain. As a result of my size, I was never very athletic. As a boy I skated like crazy, rode my bike for many miles each day, and played ball with other non-athletes. As an adult I loved tennis, golf for fun, and hiking. Football and basketball never became passions of mine. I regret this because in Kentucky this is almost the unpardonable sin.

As the rumors of the conversations about the need for a younger minister who could play football with the boys and be part of basketball tournaments in the Family Life Center, it confirmed some of my feelings that it was time to make an exit from Broadway. I had once read in a book on retirement advice that went something like this: "It takes insight and maturity to know when to get off the train. It takes courage to do it." In consultation with some of the church leaders, it was decided against an exit during the Thanksgiving, Advent, and Christmas season. Thus, about six months in advance, I announced my retirement as of January 31, 2001. I knew it was the right thing to do and future events proved this to be the case.

ON A LIGHTER NOTE

Pine Street in Richmond, Virginia, was in a declining neighborhood known as Oregon Hill. Many of the members of the congregation had once been residents but had moved to the suburbs. The church operated a "Baptist Center" which offered many services, including a food pantry, for people in need. There were many fine people living in Oregon Hill; they were simply people with limited means and limited opportunities. One of those residents was our friendly neighborhood alcoholic (we'll call him Tony). He had never really caused any major problems and always spoke to me when we passed on the street. One day my secretary announced that he had come to see me. He was reasonably sober that day and we had a pleasant conversation. Then he said, "I would like to join your church." I told him we would be happy to have him but first I needed to talk to him about his problem. "What problem?" he said. "Tony, it would not be a good witness for either you or our church for people to see you staggering around the neighborhood. We could arrange for you to get some help with your drinking problem and all I need to know is that you would be willing to begin to deal with it." Tony thought for a few moments before replying with: "Well, I 'spect I'll just join the Methodist Church." The Methodist Church was located behind Pine Street facing the next street over and the pastor was one of my good friends. He never talked with that pastor about membership. Whenever I saw Tony I would ask him if he wanted to talk further with me but assured me with, "I'm doing fine."

KIDS SAY THE DARNDEST THINGS!

The above is the title of a book written by Art Linkletter based on his interview with children on the now forgotten "House Party" TV show. I did not need to read that book to know the truth of its title. Mark was quite small when I was pastor at Vine Run and he and Pat were stranded in the parsonage for most of Tuesday through Friday when I attended seminary (we only had one car). TV watching was on the daily agenda. One Sunday morning, the teacher of Mark's Sunday School class told Pat that the highlight of her class that day was hearing Mark sing one of the beer commercial songs from his TV watching. A more public pronouncement later came from Michael when he was only five or six years old. Following the morning service, when I went to the narthex to greet people as they were leaving, Michael would come and stand beside me, usually without uttering a word. One Sunday an elderly woman stood in front of me, looked down at Michael and said, "Oh, what a beautiful picture this would make!" Then she leaned over and said to Michael, "I bet you just love church!" He looked up and loudly replied, "I hate it!" The lovely picture suddenly went out of focus but the heart of a minister's son had spoken. He wanted to sit with his mother and father just like everyone else did when they came to church. He also knew there were many times I could not do something with the family because I had a commitment at the church. With your children, nothing takes the place of presence.

YOU NEVER KNOW WHAT'S COMING DOWN THE PIKE

Roger Lamb asked me in a telephone conversation last year, if I remembered coming to him one Wednesday night with a complaint from the groom at the prior weekend's wedding rehearsal. I didn't so he told me the story. "You informed me the husband had called with the complaint that, at the rehearsal, the organist had called his bride a "_____" (censored)." Roger talked with Jennie following the rehearsal and she replied as I knew she would, "Absolutely not!" So began the investigation. Jennie kept a tape recorder on the organ during rehearsals so that she would have a record of any instructions or service changes the minister might tell the rehearsal participants. Roger, Jennie, and the soloist for the wedding all listened to the tape – twice. They then arranged to visit the home of the couple. Roger said they had a calm discussion as he relayed this message to the couple: "It is true that someone at the wedding called your wife a "_____" (censored). Jennie was not the person who said it. It was one of your bridesmaids." And thus ended another episode representing only one of the many "unusuals" that can come your way when you deal with people.

MANY TIMES, IGNORANCE IS NOT BLISS

While I was pastor at Broadway, I received a request asking if I would like to do a pulpit exchange with a pastor in England. I have forgotten exactly from where the invitation came, but I accepted. It was to be a three-week commitment and another couple arranged to go with us. (They were only able to stay for the first week and had to return due to a family crisis.) It was the exchange of pulpits as well as cars and houses. It seemed like an excellent arrangement and everything went well except for a couple of things – one relatively private and the other all too public.

A couple from the church invited us for dinner and, of course, we accepted. The red flags waved early in the evening. The hostess bragged that none of her cups or saucers matched and that she and her husband lived the simple life. She then asked how much our church gave to missions. I gave her that figure as well as supplying information about the numerous mission projects in which our church was engaged. I also gave her some information on the generosity of many of our members in both time and money with many charitable organizations in the city. In the course of the dinner, she mentioned that one of the faculty members at Southern was one of their good friends. He was also one of the pastor's friends and had preached several times in their church. He was active in the group that was attempting to take over the convention. I knew for a fact that he had "spies" planted in many of the classrooms to record anything professors might say that could be used to prove how liberal the seminary was. I also knew he was no fan of Broadway's and that I was not on his acceptable pastors' list. I was distressed about the reason but glad that our friends had to return to Louisville. It seemed like a setup, but what happened next was simply due to my ignorance.

In my second sermon, I quoted Leslie Weatherhead. At the mention of that name, I could feel the curtain come down. I was later told that he was considered a heretic and that the pastor as well as the seminary professor who had preached condemned him in their sermons. When I got back home I counted the number of books on my shelf by Weatherhead: there were eight. One of them was titled *The Christian Agnostic* in which Weatherhead left open the door for the possibility of reincarnation (it does not happen to be one in my list of possibilities). For too many Christians, if they discover one idea or teaching that they consider off base, they refuse to read or listen to anything else the person has to say. Weatherhead has written so many excellent books and has made a major contribution in his classic brief book *The Will of God*.[54] (That may have been the book from which I quoted.) No one else has ever produced a book that provides such a sound biblical basis or a more pastoral and helpful book on this great mystery. His chapter titles are: God's Intentional Will; God's Circumstantial Will; God's Ultimate Will; Discerning the Will of God; In His Will Is Our Peace. In these fifty-six pages you will find as much comfort, reassurance, and peace as you will ever discover anywhere else. It is a book that has eased many an aching heart and calmed many a troubled spirit.

WE ARE ALWAYS RESPONSIBLE FOR KEEPING OUR INNER FIRE BURNING

Far too many of the ministers I have known who boasted of being "on fire for the Lord" later experienced what they called "burn out." It is impossible to keep giving without taking the time for restocking the resources in your own life that enable you to be the kind of person who has something to offer others. You simply

---

54 Leslie Weatherhead, *The Will of God* (Nashville: Abingdon Press, 1914).

cannot be "on" twenty-four seven. No one would expect to play in a football game without the training, practice, and personal regimen that makes one physically and emotionally prepared for the game. Just so, in the ministry I discovered that much needed to be done to keep one spiritually, physically, mentally, and emotionally ready for each day's demands. Of course, the reality is always that some days we are more ready than others. Our humanity keeps us from ever achieving "perfect readiness" but some things enable us to be ready to the best our ability.

One of my basic guidelines was to find each day things that would enrich my mind, speak to my heart, and warm my soul. Much of this had to begin in the quiet of the morning before the phone began to ring and the "to do" list appeared on my desk. I always began my morning by reading a portion of Scripture. I ended my reading and devotional time with the Scriptures and Prayers for the day from *The Divine Hours* compiled by Phyllis Tickle.[55] It is a three-volume set with material for morning, midday, vespers, and night. Brief selections of Scripture offer gems from the entire Bible and prayers form the basis for our own prayers. Here is the concluding prayer for each morning (from *Prayers for Summertime):*

> Lord God, almighty and everlasting Father, you have brought me in safety to this new day: Preserve me your mighty power, that I may not fall into sin, nor be overcome by adversity; and in all I do direct me to the fulfilling of your purpose; through Jesus Christ our Lord.[56]

This morning, the prayer appointed for the week was from *Prayers for Summertime*:

> O God, the protector of all who trust in you,
> without whom nothing is strong, nothing is holy:
> Increase and multiply upon all your faithful people
> your mercy; that, with you are our ruler and guide,

---

55 Phyllis Tickle, *The Divine Hours* (New York: Doubleday, 2000).
56 Ibid, 3.

we may so pass through things temporal,
that we lose not the things eternal;
through Jesus Christ our Lord,
who live and reigns with you and the Holy Spirit,
our God, for ever and ever. Amen.[57]

On the front blank pages of the book, I note Scriptures that have especially spoken to me. A couple of examples:

John 15:9 – *I have loved you just as the Father has loved me (NJB)*. My comment: This is the way Jesus loves us! This incredible love needs to become the anchor that lets us know where we stand in relationship to our Lord. It ties directly into Paul's declaration in Romans 8:39 – *...nothing in all creation will ever be able to separate us from the love of God that is revealed in Christ Jesus our Lord.*

Psalm 103:14 – *For he understands how weak we are; he knows that we are dust (NLT)*. My note is: God remembers what we should remember! In all that we do it is necessary to keep our humanity in mind. We are not super saints. We are not super pastors. We are not super anything! God knows this and it is a source of great encouragement to remember it.

I have already cited some history and non-fiction books that remain on my reading list but I always include each day one book that is "faith oriented". Most are new finds but some are my treasured prior reads, like Wayne Oates' *The Struggle to Be Free*. It is an autographed copy with a personal note from Wayne to Pat and me. It is one of my treasures because I hear his voice in every line I read:

For me, life has from the first been a struggle. From my earliest memory I have contended with adversaries of superior number and strength. I have offered obstinate resistance to forces of constraint and sought to escape from those forces that constricted my freedom. You ask: "Freedom to do what?" Freedom to decide my own destiny; freedom to choose my own direction; freedom to express my own thoughts; freedom

---

57 Ibid, 282.

to work in my own way; freedom to put into action what God has destined that I be and become.[58]

Sometimes my inspirational reading comes from unusual places. My current novel-mystery read is *Birds of a Feather* by Jacqueline Winspear.[59] It is a book that warms your soul because of its compassion and understanding of the human situation and its suggestions for how to live redemptively.

> Maisie did not reply but simply smiled. It had been her remarkable intuitive powers along with a sharp intellect, that had led Maurice Blanche to accept her as his pupil and later as his assistant in the work he described as, "the forensic science of the whole person."[60]
>
> Billy opened his notebook and began to speak, but Maisie silenced him with a hand gently placed on his arm and a finger to her lips. "No, not now. Allow the information we've gathered to sit and stew for a while." [61]
>
> "So you put the milk in *after* the tea," said Stratton.
>
> "The old London way, Inspector Stratton: Never put the milk in first because you might waste some. If you put it in last, you can tell exactly how much you really need."[62]
>
> They were both silent for several moments. Maurice suggested a walk to the orchard. Fortunately, Maisie had dressed with such an excursion in mind, knowing Maurice's maxim: "To solve a problem, take it for a walk."[63]
>
> There was only one way to still her thoughts and racing heart, and that was to secure dominion over her body in meditation. She took four long breaths through her nose, placed her hands on her knees with the thumb and forefinger of each hand touching, and half closed her eyes. Maisie endeavored to banish all thought. Slowly the stillness of the room embraced

---

58 Wayne Oates, *The Struggle to be Free* (Philadelphia: The Westminster Press, 1983), 11.
59 Jacqueline Winspear, *Birds of a Feather* (New York: Soho Press, 2015).
60 Ibid, 9.
61 Ibid, 26.
62 Ibid, 61.
63 Ibid, 105.

her being, and the heartbeat that had been so frantic seemed to become one with her breath.[64]

My comment: Too many in this frantic culture appear to have forgotten the wisdom of Psalm 46:10 – *Be still, and know that I am God!*

One of the important ways to keep the inner fire burning is to be with people who make you feel alive! Sadly, as one gets older, many of those people are no longer around. I miss so many of them. I especially miss Perry Bramlett, our visits to used book stores, and our luncheon conversations about what we had found. He lived in a wide world of exploration and discovery about literature, history, theology, people, and ideas. His knowledge and writing about C. S. Lewis were exceptional. In most of the interims I led, I invited Perry to do "A Weekend With C. S. Lewis." The response to all his workshops was the same: "We need to have Perry back again." During our time together, I could always envision the rekindling of my motivation and commitment.

Vacations, restful times at a lake, hiking through the woods, attending inspirational and educational seminars, sightseeing in a place with beautiful vistas, or just sitting on a backyard deck watching the birds and squirrels can all be refreshing and renewing. We have to find out the things that work best for us and make certain they are incorporated into our schedules.

PLEASE, NO PERIODS!

I never liked the phase "and now in conclusion" because it indicated closure. Something was coming to an end and often I wanted it to continue. In *Finnegans Wake,* James Joyce ends the story in mid-sentence with no punctuation or explanation. (This reference comes from Robert Fulghum's fifteenth anniversary revision of his classic *All I Really Need to Know I Learned in Kinder-*

---

64 Ibid, 72.

garten).[65] I have often said that I want to leave this world with a comma marking the middle of a sentence. My dream is to continue that sentence in a place where there are no periods, only commas and one never writes "the end," only "to be continued." I have pictured "the Father's House" that Jesus talks about in John 14 as just that kind of place.

Maya Angelou made this comment in response to a question from Bryan Gumbel on an NBC Today Show: "I'm trying to be a Christian, which is no small matter. I mean it – I'm always amazed…when people walk up to me and say, 'I'm a Christian.' I always think, 'Already? You've already got it? My goodness.'"[66]

I like to think of myself as a work in progress. There is so much yet to be done! This world continues to look to me like the place for beginnings. I don't believe God is finished with any of us yet. All the promises of Scripture echo God's love and faithfulness and commitment never to abandon us. Matthew 28:20 has always been one of my favorite verses with what I call "The Great Promise". Jesus' benediction to us is: *"I am with you always."* That "always" for me implies continued learning, growing, and becoming. And who knows what blessings and marvels are wrapped up in the living quarters being prepared for us "in the Father's House" (John 14)?

---

[65] Robert Fulghum, *All I Really Need to Know I Learned in Kindergarten* (New York: Ballantine Books, 2003), 2.
[66] Maya Angelou, *NBC Today Show* (*Homiletics Journal,* November, 1997) 36.

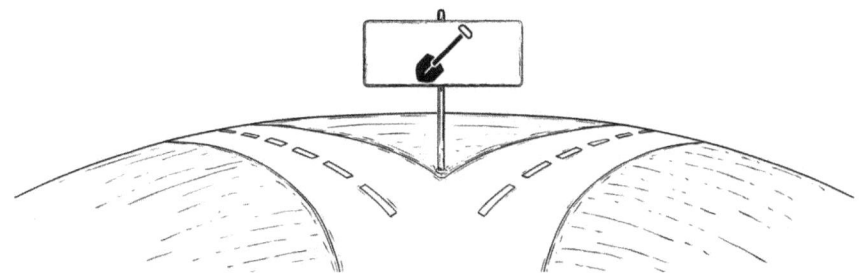

Bibliography of Quoted Sources

Alberta, Tim. *The Kingdom, the Power, and the Glory.* New York: Harper, 2003.

Alter, Robert. *The Hebrew Bible: A Translation With Commentary.* New York: W. W. Norton & Company, 2019.

Angelou, Maya. *NBC Today Show. Homiletics Journal,* 1997.

Baier, Bret. *To Rescue the Constitution: George Washington and the Fragile American Experiment.* New York: Mariner Books, 2023.

Box, C. J. *Wolf Pack.* New York: G. P. Putnam's Sons, 2019.

Breyer, Stephen. *Reading the Constitution: Why I Chose Pragmatism, Not Textualism.* New York: Simon & Schuster, 2024.

Chernow, Ron. *Alexander Hamilton.* New York: Penguin Books, 2005.

Collier, Winn. *A Burning in My Bones.* Colorado Springs: Waterbrook, 2021.

Cruden, Alexander. *Cruden's Complete Concordance.* Philadelphia: The John C. Winston Co., 1949.

Decker, Bernadette & Jonathan Montaldo, eds. *The Prayer of the Heart.* Louisville: Fons Vitae, 2003).

Drury, Bob and Tom Clavin. *Valley Forge.* New York: Simon and Schuster; 2018.

Ellis, Joseph. *American Dialogue: The Founders and Us.* New York: Alfred E. Knoph, 2018.

_____. *First Family: Abigail and John Adams.* New York: Vintage Books, 2010.

_____. *His Excellency: George Washington.* New York: Vintage Books, 2017.

Finch, Charles. *An Old Betrayal.* New York: Minotaur Books, 2013.

Frank, Charles Thompson, ed. *The New Chain-Reference Bible.* Indianapolis: B. B. Kirkbridge Bible Co., 1934.

Fulghum, Robert. *All I Need to Know I Learned in Kindergarten.* New York: Ballantine Books, 2003.

Goldberg, Phillip. *Roadsigns on the Spiritual Path.* Bolder, CO.: Sentient Publications, 2006.

Grinspan, Jon. *Wide Awake: The Forgotten Force that Elected Lincoln and Spurred the Civil War.* New York: Bloomsbury Publishing, 2024.

Hart, David Bentley. *Atheist Delusions.* New Haven: Yale University Press, 2009.

_____. *The New Testament.* New Haven: Yale University Press, 2017.

Haught, John F. *God and the New Atheism.* Louisville: Westminster John Knox Press, 2008.

Higdon, Ronald. Cleveland, TN: Parson's Porch Books.

_____. *But if Not,* 2011.

_____. *From Fear to Faith*, 2011.

_____. *In the Meantime*, 2011.

Higdon, Ronald. Gonzalez, FL., Energion Press.

_____. *Aging is Not Optional: How We Handle it Is*, 2020.

_____. *All I Need to Know I'm Still Learning at 80*, 2017.

_____. *Building Bridges in a World of Crumbling Connections*, 2022.

_____. *Finding Stability in Uncertain Times*, 2020.

_____. *Halo and Hoverboard Not Required*, 2024.

_____. *In Changing Times*, 2014.

_____. *Quitting is Never the Only Option*, 2024.

_____. *Surviving a Son's Suicide*, 2014.

_____. *Why Doesn't God Do Something?* 2017.

_____. *Wonder Where the Wonder Went*, 2021.

Hitchens, Christopher, Richard Dawkins, Sam Harris, and Daniel Dennet. *The Four Horsemen*. New York: Random House, 2019.

Johnson, Paul. *Churchill*. New York: Viking, 2009.

Kidd, Thomas S. *Benjamin Franklin: The Religious Life of a Founding Father*. New Haven: Yale University Press, 2017.

Larson, Eric. *Demon of Unrest*. New York: Crown, 2024.

_____. *The Splendid and the Vile: A Saga of Churchill, Family, and Defiance During the Blitz*. New York: Crown, 2022.

Lattimore, Richard. *The New Testament*. New York: North Point Press, 1996.

Lidsky, Isaac. *Eyes Wide Open*. New York: A TarcherPerigeeBook, 2017.

Oates, Wayne. *The Struggle to be Free*. Philadelphia: The Westminster Press, 1983.

Peterson, Eugene. *Leap Over a Wall*. New York: Harper San-Francisco, 1997.

_____, *The Message*. Colorado Springs: Navpress, 2002.

Roberts, Andrew. *Churchill: Walking With Destiny*. New York: Penguin Books, 2018.

Sayers, Dorothy. *The Unpleasantness at the Bellona Club*. London: Hodder and Stoughton, 2003.

Tey, Josephine. *The Man in the Queue*. New York: A Touchstone Book, 2007.

_____. *To Love and Be Wise*. New York: Scribner Paperback Fiction, 38.

Tickle, Phyllis. *The Divine Hours*. New York: Doubleday, 2000.

Todd, Charles. *No Shred of Evidence*. New York: William Morrow, 2016.

Vowell, Sarah. *Lafayette in the Somewhat United States*. New York: Riverhead Books, 2015.

Weatherhead, Leslie. *The Will of God*. Nashville: Abingdon Press, 1914.

Weber, Karl, ed. *Lincoln: A President for the Ages*. New York: Alfred E. Knoph, 2018.

Widmer, Ted. *Lincoln on the Verge: Thirteen Days to Washington.* New York: Simon and Schuster Paperbacks, 2020.

Winspear, Jacqueline. *Birds of a Feather.* New York: Soho Press, 2015.

———. *Maisie Dobbs.* Soho Press, 2003.

www.ingramcontent.com/pod-product-compliance
Lightning Source LLC
Chambersburg PA
CBHW030943090426
42737CB00007B/518